Living an
INTUITIVE Life

Awaken to a Soul Led Life

Guided by Your Intuition

Living an INTUITIVE Life

Awaken to a Soul Led Life

Guided by Your Intuition

RAISE
THE VIBE
BOOKS

By: Liz Peterson

First Printing: 2025

eBook- ISBN: 979-8-9870619-5-4

Paperback- ISBN: 979-8-9870619-6-1

Library of Congress Control Number: 2025924961

Comments and inquiries regarding this book may be sent to the author at www.raisethevibewithliz.com

For updates and information, please follow: @ raisethevibewithliz on social media

Published by Liz Peterson /

Raise The Vibe Books, LLC.

Vashon, WA 98070

Proofreader/editing: FIVVER, Lillian M

Book layout and design: Liz Peterson

Cover design: Liz Peterson

Book Cover design: FIVVER, sam_4321

Back Cover Photo: Rick Dahms

For the Empowerment
of the reader

Also by Liz Peterson

Mom died last night:
My shared death experience

Sex magic:
How to use sexual energy to manifest your
dreams

Cliteracy and The Yoni Egg

Yoni Diary:
A companion to Cliteracy and The Yoni Egg

Table of Contents

Introduction

My entire life, I struggled with trusting my intuition. If you're reading this book, I'm sure you know those moments where something happens and you think, "I just had that thought," or "I knew that," or "If I'd only listened," as you shake your head once more, your palm going to your forehead or you roll your eyes yet again. Whether it's moments beforehand or much earlier, it happens... and has happened your whole life, often. This was me.

I also went back and forth about whether I was, quote, "normal" (as society puts it), or whether I truly had extrasensory gifts. When the magic, what I call it happened, I was thrilled and felt like I finally had proof. But then I'd think, "Nah," and blow it off as a fluke. I was steeped in cultural expectations and living a normal, everyday life through adolescence, my 20s, and marriage while raising children. Yet at the same time, I was having out of the ordinary experiences. From sensing the energy of a room or the emotional state of a person, to knowing something was going to happen before it happened, to feeling a disembodied presence nearby those moments were anything but ordinary or "normal," as we like to categorize them.

Time after time, life would prove these things to me through different occurrences, but still, I didn't trust my intuition, my gifts, or myself fully and I didn't listen. Until one day in late August 2011, when my family and I suffered a devastating house fire. It wasn't the actual fire or the loss itself that made me begin trusting myself, believing, and finally having faith in my intuition. It was what happened before the fire even started.

One afternoon, a week before the fire, I was sitting on our deck relaxing in the sunshine while my children played. All of a sudden, out of nowhere, I was jolted back to awareness shocked with a profound thought or knowing. I sprung from my relaxed, lounging state to sitting fully upright. I was struck with an overwhelming feeling that something terrible was going to happen, and it filled every cell of my being. I gasped as I sat there, fully alert. Being a mother, my first thought was my children. I took a deep breath with my eyes closed and thought, "Please not my children," as I opened my gaze to the sky. With that, I took a deep inhale, rose from my seat, and went inside to share the experience with my (then) husband. After telling him, I let it drift to the back of my mind, except for the occasional haunting thought that would creep in. No other information followed that initial feeling of doom.

Now it's a week later, the day before the first day of school. I was moving through the house doing my usual daily to-do list: pick up, clean up, laundry. The kids were playing outside. I cleaned up the kitchen after breakfast, picked up the floors, and started the laundry as usual. Then something interesting began to happen. As I followed my thoughts, I noticed they weren't the usual task-oriented thoughts I typically had. I started getting unusual ideas. Suddenly, the thought "Back up your computer" popped into my head. So, I thought, Huh, okay, and followed through, starting the backup on the external hard drive before moving on to another task.

When the backup finished, I grabbed the hard drive and walked into the kitchen to toss it into the drawer like I normally did but I froze, hovering above the drawer. Out of nowhere, the thought came: "Put it in the back bedroom, in a dresser drawer or the closet." I stood there pondering the thought for a moment, wondering why I'd do that. Then I didn't listen. I tossed the hard drive into the kitchen drawer.

This continued happening all day. One thought after another. Some things I followed through on, and some I dismissed. One of the things I ignored happened in the hallway closets on the main floor: one was for coats, the other for linens. Walking through the hallway, I suddenly got the idea to take everything from the linen closet and move it downstairs. I stopped, opened the bi-fold doors, and looked at the shelves. As I stared, I stepped back and thought, "Why would I move this stuff downstairs? That's silly." I closed the doors and moved on.

I was also moved to do all the laundry in the house. I finished and put away every load except one: my husband's work clothes, left in the dryer until morning.

Another odd thing happened that day. I was at the landing at the bottom of the stairs outside the doors to the laundry room and the downstairs hallway. As I bent down to grab a basket of laundry, I saw someone walk by in my peripheral vision, heading down the hall. Without looking, I said, "Could you carry this upstairs so I can grab the other basket?" thinking it was one of my sons. When I got no response, I peeked around the door frame. No one was there. I knew I'd seen someone, so I even walked to the end of the hallway toward the bathroom. Nothing. Huh. That's weird, I thought, grabbing the basket and heading upstairs. I wondered if it had been a spirit, maybe one of the former owners who had passed on.

The next morning, after my older children had left for school, I walked down the hallway and told my 4 and 7-year-olds to get dressed and ready, then went to the kitchen. I grabbed the older kids' dishes from the dining table and walked into the galley kitchen. There was a window above the sink that looked out to the side yard and the breezeway that connected the house to the garage. The garage door also had a window.

As I stood washing dishes, something flashed in the garage door window across from me. I looked up quickly and saw a flash of fire inside the doorway on the left-hand side where the light switch was. I stopped washing dishes, yelled for the kids, and called 911. While talking to the operator, it dawned on me that even though the fire was in the garage beside the house, we needed to get out immediately. I rushed the boys and myself out grabbing nothing but my truck keys. I didn't think to take anything: our pets, my purse, the computer, my son's backpack... nothing. A part of me thought I wouldn't need to because the fire was in the garage and help was on the way. Even when my first grader asked if he should grab his backpack, I told him no. Little did I know having only lived on the island for nine months, how different things were here. And little did I know how fast that fire would spread.

Sitting in the truck, backed away from the house, we watched and waited for the fire department. We saw the fire travel across the breezeway and into the main house. It was fast, destructive, and devastating.

Fast forward to the end of the fire... The fire destroyed most of the top floor, the kitchen, dining, living room, upstairs hallway, and bathroom. The rest of the house suffered smoke and water damage, including all bedrooms and the downstairs family playroom. It was overwhelming. I felt shock, grief, and a strange sense of violation. But I also felt extremely blessed that my family, and my children were safe.

After the smoke settled and I was allowed to walk through the house, I suddenly realized I had been guided the day before to save things from the fire. If I had put the hard drive in the back bedroom dresser or closet instead of the kitchen drawer, I would still have the computer's contents especially my youngest child's baby photos. If I had moved my memory boxes, poetry, writings, blankets, keepsakes, and my son's beloved baby calendar like I'd been guided to do and put them in the downstairs storage closet, I would still have them today.

That last load of laundry, my husband's work clothes left in the dryer... saved and ready for him to keep supporting us.

And that white figure I saw walk past the laundry room? I believe it was either one of the previous owners or another spirit trying to warn me. I had never seen a spirit inside the house until that day, though I had sensed something outside before.

Looking back now, I understand that Spirit knew my only focus in that moment would be getting my children to safety that I wouldn't grab a single thing. Spirit was guiding me the day before, trying to help me save what I could from the blaze.

What I learned from this experience was to finally believe in and fully trust my intuition. To stop blowing it off. To listen.

I decided that from that day onward, I would pay attention to the guidance I was given. Of course, I was a work in progress, and from that point forward it took practice. Practicing, working on listening, paying attention, and acting on what I received. I began to pay attention to what popped into my mind and actually follow through on it. Acknowledging and trusting that I was being guided that the guidance was there to help me in situations I didn't even know were happening yet, in situations that were about to unfold, or in things occurring within seconds or days of the thought. Guidance that nudged me to pay attention to what was coming or showed me things that would benefit me. I realized that those little thoughts that popped into my mind were not random; they were guiding me in a beneficial direction, helping me navigate my life.

And that's what I began to do. Every time I got an idea, I followed it.

I call it following the threads, or following the breadcrumbs. It's listening to my gut, paying attention to my thoughts; it's following my inner guidance system, my "inner compass" which I now literally have tattooed on my arm. I know now that it's always guiding me to the next best thing at any given moment. That I always have everything I need exactly when I need it. All I have to do is listen. And follow through.

Now, I'm human, I didn't start following it 100% of the time right away. I wish! I still looked for signs, for validation, for proof, or I wouldn't act immediately. In the beginning, I kicked myself often for ignoring the guidance, haha. It took time, and it took practice. And the biggest part was learning to follow through every single time.

I believe we are all gifted with this inner guidance system. We are directly connected to what Buddha called Indra's Web, a web or field of information, much like the world wide web. We have access to information past, present, and future. And I believe we have a team of helpers on the other side guiding us at all times.

Allow me to take this a step deeper: I believe we, our soul is a fractal of Source Consciousness, a part of the whole. If we are Source Consciousness, then we have access to all that is, was, and will be. When we reach what I call Soul Embodiment - where the big S Soul self has blended with the small s physical self - we become Consciousness experiencing life. Source experiencing life through us, as us, for us. So of course we have access to everything in existence, in all dimensions of time. Being of the web of life gives us a constant stream of intel.

Whether you believe we have a team of helpers on the other side assisting us, or that we have access to a universal field of information that we can tap into, or both – whatever our belief, Spirit wants to help us. Spirit wants to help you. And for me, after the fire, I know Spirit definitely tried to help me - whatever label or belief you choose to attach to it.

I also believe everyone should be taught to trust these gut instincts, these inclinations, our intuition. There was a time in history when these skills were taught. We had to listen to survive. I think we lost these abilities when we became "civilized," when life became less about survival, though of course survival is still very real for many. But in that shift, we lost valuable generational knowledge about our inherent gifts of knowing and how to follow them.

Now, as we move through a shift in consciousness on the planet becoming once again connected to the earth, the cosmos, and emerging out of separation consciousness, we're realizing we are not separate from the whole but part of it. We are remembering who we are. We are once again learning how to be in flow with life, and with all that is. Because not only are we part of life itself, we are part of the greater consciousness creating our lives through divine inspiration. Life is always guiding us if we are listening.

So, listen to those thoughts that pop into your mind, the words spoken to you, the images shown to you. Follow your gut feelings and your internal knowing's - your inner guidance. That guidance is leading you through your life if you allow it; it's there to help you and benefit you. Always guiding you to the next best thing.

I'm hoping that sharing my story can help you. Maybe you're resonating with what I'm sharing. Maybe this can help you learn to trust yourself, follow your guidance, and begin following through on it as well.

You will not be disappointed. When you choose to live this way, you discover a life filled with synchronicities, coincidences, and what I call flow state. A divine orchestration of events begins to unfold organically, everything falling into place in divine timing and perfect occurrence. A thought of a friend - who then calls you. A thought of an idea - that becomes a new career. A thought of an event - that then happens. A nudge to take care of something that ends up helping you in an unforeseen way.

You find yourself in a dance with the universe - in co-creation with the Divine, with Source Consciousness.

The Universe itself providing you with everything you need and desire... and even things you didn't know you needed until they arrived, things that turn out to be better than you could have ever imagined.

What Is Intuition?

What is intuition? Well, the first thing I want to say is that everybody has it. We're all born with it, and you are already using it. If you don't feel like you're aware of it, or you're not sure you're using it, you can begin to develop that awareness and train it, hone your skills. And if you are aware of your intuition already, you can develop it further and strengthen it.

Webster's Dictionary has a great definition of intuition. It says, *"Intuition is the ability to understand something immediately, without the need for conscious reasoning,"* and *"a thing one knows or considers likely from instinct rather than conscious reasoning."*

For me, intuition is a gut feeling, an internal felt sense, a vision, a message heard, or a knowing that arises. You know that aha moment when puzzle pieces suddenly fall into place in your mind? Or that feeling you get in the pit of your stomach when something is right or when something is just off. When something feels right to me, I often feel a sense of wellbeing. Or when I know or feel the truth of something, I might get goosebumps. I call them truth bumps. The bigger the truth, the bigger the bumps. Mine usually begin up my spine and sometimes travel into the back of my neck. And when that truth is divine truth that ring the bell, right on the money kind of truth, I get chills throughout my entire body, like someone just turned up truth's volume.

When something is wrong, I might experience an aversion to it, or instinctively lean back. I might get an ache in my stomach, or suddenly think, "Hmm... that's not right."

If it's a thought like that, I've learned it's my inner knowing, a message received through an instant thought in the moment, a psychic knowing. Sometimes I get a picture or a little movie in my mind. Sometimes I smell something, or hear a snippet of a song. Sometimes I overhear the exact words I need, see just the right phrase somewhere, or notice repeating numbers on a clock like 11:11, 4:44, 5:55, 10:10, or 12:12 always catching them in perfect timing.

Intuition goes by many names: guidance, inner guidance system, inner GPS, inner compass, intuition, insight, foresight, instinct, gut feeling, a hunch, ESP (extrasensory perception), or a sixth sense to name a few. There's also what I consider the outer guidance system, where you're tapped into the collective mind or collective energy and receive messages from outside sources - friends, strangers, media, or divinity itself.

Spirit uses people and platforms to relay messages to you all the time.

We receive this sensory input through our physical body, our nervous system, and our energetic body or biofield - our aura, chakras, energy system. We use our five senses and our extrasensory perception. These systems pull information from your surroundings and from the people around you. It's far beyond the five senses. Yes, we use them to read our environment, but intuition extends into our psychic sense's - clairvoyance, clairaudience, clairsentience, claircognizance, and clairgustance or clairalience.

There was a time when societies relied primarily on intuition. But over the centuries, Western society shifted toward intellect, logic, reasoning, and scientific inquiry as the preferred way to understand the world, deeming it unreliable. This devalued intuition and undermined our trust in it, causing a disconnection from emotion, the greater experience of life, and the unseen or metaphysical aspects of our existence. As a society, we choose the material aspects of life over the spiritual ones.

Science says intuition is the unconscious mind rapidly analyzing patterns from past experiences, knowledge, and information to generate a conclusion or feeling about the present moment or circumstance. That our senses are constantly scanning our environment to keep us safe and secure. These are both true, but it has more to do with logic and conscious reasoning and are more analytical and intellectual in nature. Adjacent to intuition as I know it, which I feel is Spirit led and lies in our connection to Consciousness or. shall I say, rooted in us being a part of Universal Consciousness.

Albert Einstein famously said, *"The intuitive mind is a sacred gift and the rational mind is a faithful servant. We have created a society that honors the servant and has forgotten the gift."*

Intuition is not based in fear. Fear is an action of the amygdala in the brain, which triggers the body's stress response - fight, flight, freeze, or fawn response. Intuition is calm and direct. Fear is loud, anxious, and panicked. Intuition doesn't question; we do. That questioning is fear and ego. Ego is fear based, seeks external validation, and is tied to the past. Intuition is wisdom based; it speaks self-acceptance and love. It is not ego driven or self-serving; its answers are rooted in love, goodness, and the good of all.

When we pose a question, intuition gives the answer before we even finish asking the question. It is ego and self-doubt that immediately question that answer. If we've gone beyond the initial answer, that's fear talking – our own uncertainty within ourselves, doubt and fears of being wrong or making the wrong.

Intuition is linked to the pineal gland, a small endocrine gland located in the center of the brain. In spiritual and metaphysical traditions, the pineal gland is called the "third eye," seen as a gateway to higher consciousness, spiritual awakening, and heightened intuition. Practices such as meditation, visualization, and breathwork are used to open and activate the pineal gland, leading to increased intuitive ability. The third eye is associated with inner wisdom and psychic abilities, and it releases hormones like melatonin and DMT, which can induce altered states of consciousness.

Intuition is your inherent instinct. Instincts are automatic behaviors triggered by stimuli that lead to a physical response. Think of a deer in the wild. As a prey animal, when it's grazing or standing in a field, it suddenly lifts its head because its internal alert system senses danger. Something in its environment has triggered an instinctual response. It "senses" it.

Just like the deer, you have this instinctual knowing encoded within you from birth. We are wired for it. We are walking antennae tuned into our environment, people, places, and things - receivers and transmitters of a constant flow of information. As Bruce Lipton points out, we have a trillion cells in our body, each cell acting like an energy receptor that receives and processes environmental signals. Essentially our cells are reacting to energetic signals, like vibrational frequencies and, when activated, trigger a series of events within the cells of our being.

You've experienced this when you suddenly sense that someone is staring at you and you look up and catch them. You might be at the grocery store, minding your own business, and suddenly you look up to find someone across the produce section looking your way. Their energy has impressed upon you, interacted with your energy field, just like the deer sensing a predator.

This happens to me all the time whether with people or animals. An onlooker from across the room, a partner's ability to signal my attention – no matter where I am or what I'm doing. One day, for example, I was sunbathing on my deck, listening to music with my 4lb Chihuahua Yorkie next to me. Out of nowhere, I popped my head up to look into the field behind the house. I didn't consciously know why, but my body did. To my surprise, there they were: three coyotes just 24 feet from the edge of the deck, slinking toward us. Yikes! Thank you, instinct.

Source Consciousness and Spirit also have access to different channels with which to reach us. We're tapped into the collective mind and collective energy. As previously mentioned, we receive messages via friends, strangers, media, numbers, signs, and symbols. This is Source Consciousness - Spirit using people, words, numbers, license plates, billboards, emails, and social media to relay messages to us. The key is learning to recognize them.

We are born with intuition, can build it, and strengthen it. And it naturally evolves and grows as we do. You've heard the saying "wisdom with age." Yes, wisdom comes from experience, but intuition opens and expands as we age, too. We're seeing this now as we enter the Age of Aquarius, the shift into higher consciousness and intuitive evolution. As Consciousness rises, so do we. Intuition is a natural byproduct of this evolution in consciousness, higher level awareness and spiritual growth.

You may think, "Not me." And yes, some people are born with inherent knowing, while others need to develop their skills or simply learn to trust them. It's like piano playing: some people have a natural talent, some don't, and many fall in between. Some can learn to play Beethoven's Fifth after years of practice, and others never will. Sometimes you see a savant, instantly proficient. Like the child "born awake", birthed knowing, seeing, hearing beyond their five senses – using their sixth sense abilities to see beyond the physical material world into the otherwise unseen all around us.

We hone intuition and psychic skills through intention, attention, awareness, and practice. Whether we're born with natural sensitivity or think we aren't, we can train our intuition through awareness, attunement, and practice. You can become more aware, more in tune, and eventually find your flow state where information flows naturally and your life becomes an unfolding rather than something you force.

But how do you know? How does intuition show up?

Here are a few examples of intuition in action:

- You're at work and get the idea to give someone your business card, but you don't. The next day your colleague tells you they did and now they've been invited to an event. You realize that could have been you.
- A parent has a sudden internal knowing their child is in need or in danger. When they check, they find it's true.
- You feel or "know" something is wrong with a family member. That same day you receive a call that they're sick, had an accident, or have passed away.
- Someone pops into your mind, and moments later the phone rings, it's them.
- You dream about someone, and upon waking discover they're going through exactly what you dreamed.

These are examples of your intuition at work, ways you may be tapping into something beyond your five senses. It might show up as a gut feeling when something is wrong. It might manifest as goosebumps when something is right or in alignment. It might appear as an idea that comes out of nowhere and, when you follow through on it, ends up opening a door to a new possibility in your life.

I find it incredibly important to pay attention to our physical cues and our thoughts, because we're getting nudges, hints, ideas, and information all the time. These moments are our intuition in action. This is our inner guidance coming from our higher selves, higher wisdom, higher consciousness, oneness, "The All That Is" helping us create and co-create our lives.

This higher wisdom wants us to succeed. No matter who you are, the information presented to you is meant to lead you from one thing to the next - from one breadcrumb to another in a divine flow. It's a weave of information moving through you and then intertwining with the whole of existence. An orchestra, a divine play. For you and for the collective.

It leads you to the next lesson, the next possibility, the next job experience, the next best thing for your loved ones, and of course the next best thing for you. When you choose to live your life through your intuition through what I call "intuitive action" you begin to live a life filled with coincidence and synchronicity. You become in tune with the natural, moment-to-moment unfolding of life. You begin to have the experience of living a magical existence, one with more of the things you love and enjoy: peace, creativity, joy, fulfillment. "All your needs met, and more", more than you knew to ask for. Life begins to manifest for you rather than you having to "make" things happen. You can release the striving and instead surrender into a beautiful state of following your natural inspiration instead. Following your intuition.

Daily Meditation

Find a comfortable seat on the floor, in a chair, sitting upright in bed, or even lying down if that's what your body prefers. Take a deep breath and begin to come into your body.

Place one hand on your heart and the other on your abdomen. Gently close your eyes and breathe deeply.

Bring your attention to your palms. This will help bring you into your body, anchoring your soul self at your center. Then relax your hands on your lap and take another deep breath.

Let anything that happened before this moment, or anything that will happen after it, remain outside. Come into your center. Come fully into this present moment.

Feel yourself arriving here, bringing awareness into your center, into your solar plexus. Draw your attention fully inside your body, gathering all of your intention, attention, and awareness within.

Now bring your awareness to your grounding cord. Imagine sending it deep into the planet, all the way to the molten core of the Earth like roots reaching down, firmly anchoring you.

Draw Earth's energy up into your body, flowing through your central channel, rising up and out through the top of your head, connecting you to the All That Is. Then allow that energy to flow back down through your body and your central channel. Feel it moving up and down balancing, harmonizing, filling you with energy.

As your body fills, notice the light within you expanding. Feel it spreading through your whole being down through your toes, along your legs, up through your torso, into your arms, hands, and fingertips. Let it rise through your neck, your face, your ears, and your crown.

Now expand this energy just beyond your physical body above, below, in front, behind, and on both sides.

With your next breath, expand your energy farther until it fills your room, your space. Let it stretch outward, filling every corner of your home, your yard, your neighborhood.

Expand even more to your town, your state, your country, your continent. Let it travel across the oceans, encircling the entire planet. Your energy now wraps around the Earth, connected to all that is.

Expand just a little more. Feel the peace within this vastness no time, only space. Nothingness, and yet oneness. No separation. Just being.

If thoughts drift in, let them drift out. No need to attach to them. Allow peace and tranquility. Simply rest in your presence.

Take a deep breath and begin to return. Gently pull your energy back, drawing it from space, back through the stars, back toward the Earth.

Bring your awareness down: from the world view, to the oceans, to your continent, your country, your state. Draw your energy into your town, your yard, your home, your room, and finally back into your body. Rest in the stillness for a few minutes.

Sit with your energy now grounded, present, and peaceful. Stay here as long as you'd like, or gently transition out of the meditation when you feel ready.

Carry this grounded, peaceful presence with you into your day.

How Does Intuition Work?

For me personally, my intuition works like downloads on a computer. I receive words, phrases, images, and song lyrics in my thoughts, along with feelings and sensations in my body. These are examples of how I receive information. Everyone receives information in their own way, and it's a journey to learn how you individually receive it.

Intuition is a receptive tool that gives us personally curated tips and insights that make our lives better: our situations better, our work environments better, our families' lives better. Just beginning to listen to your guidance makes life instantly begin to shift for the better.

Whether we are dealing with adversity, health issues, work, family, or anything else from life's laundry list of possibilities, the guidance is always a positive influence. This guidance - our intuition - shows us that we are supported, whether we listen in the moment or look back later and realize we wish we had. It's when we don't, that is the issue.

So how does intuition work?

There is a field of information around you, like a sea. Like a fish in a bowl surrounded by water it's unaware of, we are immersed in a universal field of energy - the space we occupy. Information travels through this space around us, the way vibrations and sound travel through water. We are downloading and receiving information from our environment all the time, even when we're unaware of it. We could be completely unplugged from the news and media and still receive a feeling, a sense, a random thought, or an image about what's happening in the collective - the larger world.

When we are around people, our energy systems are downloading information, picking up feelings, sensations, and telepathic communications. All we need to do is begin to pay attention and cultivate a deeper awareness, acknowledging that everything we're feeling and experiencing might not be ours. I have to ask myself all the time, "Is this mine?" about what I'm thinking and feeling and often, it's not.

Think of it as data you need being input into your field of awareness. You are tapping into the Universal Field of Awareness - Spirit is downloading the content you need to succeed. You've been delivered a set of instructions to consider - presenting themselves to you to bring awareness to what you're hearing, thinking, or feeling. Although our five senses are always active, intuition goes beyond sight, smell, taste, hearing, and touch. It is an extrasensory version of those senses, and both our physical and energetic bodies are involved. Our nervous system reacts to stimuli, but our energetic field which is comprised of the chakras and biofield or aura also takes in information. Our sixth sense abilities, or ESP (extrasensory perception), reach beyond the normal range of the five physical senses to perceive information from the field of consciousness, which comprises everything, everything that was, is, and will be.

Like a radio tower that is always receiving information, we are receiving as well through our largest visible sensing organ, our bodies and our invisible sensing body, our energetic systems.

Our energetic field is like a large antenna and is connected to the larger consciousness field of the universal life field. Like antennas, we pull information from outside ourselves as well as transmit. We receive information not only through our aura or energy field or biofield as scientists call it, but through our chakra system as well.

Our instinctual senses are giving us constant information. Layered on top of those instinctual senses, our intuitive senses are also inputting information. If we are visual people, we may receive an image, a snapshot, or a little mini movie. These images may be based on our past experiences. Spirit uses what we've experienced in our lives to translate information to us. It can also be symbolic. You may see an object that has a particular meaning only to you as a way for you to comprehend what's going on.

For instance, you may see a picture of a white dove. If a white dove means peace to you, this symbol may be pointing out that an upcoming situation will be peaceful. A white dove to some might mean peace, but to others it could signify a wedding or a funeral. It depends on your point of reference. You have to learn, over time and with practice, what the symbols represent to you and what your symbols mean.

You might receive a mental flash of someone's name, their face, or a particular scene. Seeing your mother's face could mean there's going to be a situation involving your mother or someone else's. If you are a psychic medium, it could mean that your mother, or another person's mother, is stepping forward to communicate.

The information I get is based on my own life experiences people, places, and things I have encountered throughout my life. Because I receive information in this way, I've had an added lesson of differentiation. You too may receive your information in this way and have to learn this valuable lesson. I've had to continually ask myself over the years, "Is this mine?" to differentiate between what is mine and what is not in any given moment of intuitive knowing. But when I'm with a client, I know that the information being received is for them.

One time, I was working with a client who was helping his sister transition to a different living situation. Before I knew any of this, I shared with him that I was seeing in my mind's eye an apartment complex. There were small bungalows on each side lining a walkway, and at the back was a two-story building with two apartments on the bottom and two on the top. He replied, "Yes, that's my sister's apartment building." This apartment complex had been a place I'd lived when I was 20 years old. Spirit had impressed that image on me using my own memory as a visual reference point for his and his sister's situation.

Our feeling sense may present as anything physical in the body: a stomach sensation, a temperature shift, a heaviness, or even pain in a particular area if someone is sick, hurt, or injured. These intuitive sensations can apply to spaces, objects, and people - incarnate or disincarnate. If you are a psychic medium, you could be sensing all of these feelings from those across the veil, or from those who have chosen to remain close in our dimension.

You might experience a taste all of a sudden that you shouldn't be tasting like a specific food, metal, tobacco, or even blood. The same happens with smells that aren't present in your immediate environment, such as perfume, roses, smoke, cigarettes, cigars, etc. Tasting blood can be an intuitive hit that someone has been in a car accident. Smelling roses often means angels are with you. You might have a grandmother who had a rose garden, and that becomes her signal to you that she's nearby. Or you might smell your grandfather's cologne.

One time, I arrived at a women's retreat on Guemes Island and, while putting my things away in my assigned room, I smelled cigarette smoke. No one was smoking or a smoker in the house, and it was a non-smoking property, so no one was smoking outside either. When I went downstairs, I mentioned it to the women, and one of them responded, "Oh, that's my dad. I always smell smoke when he is around." We receive information from the other side through our senses of smell, taste, feeling, hearing, and psychic sight.

If you receive your information via hearing, you might hear a word, a voice - someone speaking to you in your voice or theirs, or song lyrics. I often receive messages through song lyrics. One afternoon, on the way to pick up my son from soccer practice, my phone sitting in my purse suddenly started playing a song by Kenny Wayne Shepherd. I found that interesting, considering I was almost at the pickup location, it wasn't Bluetooth connected to the car speakers, and nobody else was in the car. That same song was playing when I took him to get to-go food at a local restaurant right after practice.

When this happens, I read the song's lyrics to glean the message. When I hear a snippet of a song upon waking from sleep, I know the specific words I heard are the message. My deceased mother often communicated with me in this way after her death.

We may also hear words spoken directly to us from Spirit or a disincarnate spirit. One time I was in L.A., staying at a hotel with my family, and heard a voice say, "Wake up," in the room where I was sleeping. After my mother's death in 2022, I heard my name, "Lisbeth," called. She was one of the only people who called me by that name, and I was alone in the house.

I remember in the fall of 2017, after years of waiting to be able to clearly hear Spirit, I finally had an experience. One evening, I was driving home from a Raja yoga meditation class at East West Bookshop in Seattle. As I was driving across the West Seattle Bridge, blissed out from class, I heard a man's voice say to me, "Are you ready?" It was crystal clear, came out of nowhere, and snapped me out of my dazed state and back into conscious awareness.

If you are clairaudient, you may receive messages in your own voice or someone else's. If you're worried about having this clair ability because people might think you're "crazy," I understand. In the past, many people were put into institutions or labeled mentally ill because the ability to communicate with spirit was misunderstood. But there's no need to worry - there is a stark difference. Spiritualists and practitioners distinguish clairaudience from symptoms of mental health conditions like schizophrenia because they are able to decode information that isn't available through normal means. And a voice from true spiritual intelligence will never ask you to harm yourself, another, or a place. The Divine does no harm.

One of the ways clairaudience often begins to present is by hearing people talking as you are falling asleep. This is because, as you drift off, you enter a stage called the hypnagogic state. It is a theta brainwave state just before sleep delta state, and is also the brainwave state we are in from birth to around seven years of age. This is why children can often speak to deceased loved ones, spirits, and "invisible friends." It is also the state we're in during hypnosis and trance states - a time when there is a shift in brain activity from our left hemisphere to the right hemisphere of our brain.

You can gently experiment with this hearing sense by practicing asking questions. Ask a question and listen for the answer. It usually comes before you've even finished asking. If it comes more than a few seconds later, it is usually your ego answering. Intuitive guidance will never be bad advice or anything that would harm you or another person. And the answer may not always arrive in words right away. It may come later in the form of a song, something you overhear, a comment from a friend or loved one, or in a dream.

Intuition often shows up as thoughts. You may have the thought to try Kundalini yoga, another form of yoga, or an athletic class that would be good for your health. If you don't follow through, you may start receiving emails, suggestions from people, or see posts in your social media feed nudging you toward that same guidance. It often comes in threes.

If you're unhappy with your current living or employment situation, you may get the idea to start looking into other possibilities or applying for other jobs. You may even start to see offers appear. A few years ago, I was going to move into a tiny house, but that fell through. Through a series of interactions, I was led to the perfect place. A conversation with a friend led to a possible apartment. Just before it was time to sign the lease, the apartment owner referred me to someone who had contacted her looking for a renter. That led me to the perfect house for myself and my youngest son.

Your intuition could also show up as a knowing. This is claircognizance clear knowing. You just know things. I believe this is the least spoken about clair, and I have a theory about why. In our society, at least while I was growing up if you said, "I know," or just knew too much, you were considered a know it all. It's still often discouraged. It can be used as a bullying tactic. And as we know from Brené Brown's work, we don't want to be cast out of the village or risk not belonging, so we've learned to hold our tongues.

This goes even deeper when you consider the societal conditioning that children should be seen and not heard, or that women should be sweet, accommodating, and quiet. In the therapeutic realm, saying "I feel" instead of "I know" is often perceived as easier to hear and less triggering, so we're taught to soften the truth to pacify the egoic reactions of others.

Claircognizant people have a direct line to Consciousness Source, Divine wisdom, Spirit, spirit guides, angels, etc. all of which are aspects of Consciousness. Claircognizance appears as a thought, an idea, or a knowing. A simple example would be this: you're getting hungry and have the thought, "I want pizza." A moment later, your child or the person you're with says, "I want pizza." It's just that simple, the thought pops into your mind.

I often have single word thoughts or intuitive hits that are validated during conversations with family, friends, or loved ones. I've heard, "I was just thinking that," more times than I can count. I've had someone pop into my thoughts and then run into them later that day. I've had diagnostic words arrive in my mind that turned out to be the exact medical term a client received from their physician, or the name of an ailment they were struggling with.

You might have a person appear in your mind - either their name or their face and minutes later they call, text, or you run into them. You might overhear something and instantly know it's the answer to a question you've been asking. You may see a mental image and discover it's exactly what a friend or loved one is describing in that moment. You might listen to someone explain a pain in their back and then feel that exact pain in your own body. You may sense anxiety or a foreboding feeling and later discover your city is on high alert for an environmental or safety situation.

Claircognizance can be considered an aspect of telepathy. Telepathy is the ability to receive information in the mind - communication from mind to mind without the use of speech. It is defined as "the direct transfer of information from one mind to another without any physical or sensory interaction" -the transfer of thoughts, feelings, and images. Animals and animal communicators communicate this way. Spirits, angels, and ETs communicate through telepathy. When you have claircognizant abilities, you're receiving one side of that communication channel.

To the degree you are connected to Oneness, Source Consciousness, and the Universe, your ability to sense information also depends on your brain. Even though we use both hemispheres, we can still be left or right dominant. I have always considered myself right-brain dominant. If you are right-brain dominant, you may experience stronger intuition, creativity, emotional processing, facial recognition, spatial reasoning, artistic talent, and pattern recognition. Left-brain dominance is associated with detail-oriented tasks, fine motor skills, analytical thinking, math ability, and sequencing. Both sides communicate through the corpus callosum, the bridge between duality (left/right brain), the union of logic and intuition, conscious and subconscious, material and spiritual, and higher consciousness, wholeness - in esoteric tradition, unifying the divine feminine and divine masculine, and influencing spiritual experiences / awakening.

I recently came across Jill Bolte Taylor's TED Talk and read her book My Stroke of Insight. She is a brain scientist who had a stroke in the left hemisphere of her brain. She describes how, when this happened, her mental chatter disappeared and the barriers between herself and the world around her dissolved. She felt at one with all the energy that was around her, expansive, felt at one with everything - consciousness itself. She found nirvana. She says, and I quote:

"I can step into the consciousness of my right hemisphere, where we are the life force power of the universe. The life force power of the 50 trillion beautiful molecular geniuses that make up my form, at one with all that is. I believe that the more time we spend choosing to run the deep inner peace circuitry of our right hemispheres, the more peace we will project into the world, and the more peaceful our planet will be."

I agree wholeheartedly.

Everyone experiences intuition in their own way even though we have similarities. You receive your information through your own unique senses, with your own perceptions. It's up to us to learn how we personally receive intuitive information and what it means for ourselves and those around us. You may even find that everything that passes across your senses is, in fact, your intuitive guidance - for yourself, and those with and near you. You are receiving information constantly from people, objects you touch, your environments, areas you're in, places you sit, passersby, and energy fields. You are getting a constant stream of information at all times. All you need to do is tap in.

Tracking Practice

Now that we've explored what intuition is and how it works, it's time to put that information into practice.

What I want you to do is start paying attention to any thoughts, ideas, images, and feelings you receive from this moment forward. I recommend getting a small journal you can carry with you. I started doing this years ago, and it worked beautifully. I began noticing all the times the information I received directly correlated to things I later experienced.

Keep it in your purse, next to your bedside table, or in your car. I've also used the notepad on my phone.

You can make mental notes, but writing things down gives you proof in hand. You can look back through your journal to track your guidance and intuition and see where it manifested. I used to keep mine in my purse so it was always available. I also keep a notebook beside my bed because I've noticed recently that, as energy has sped up in the world, I get intuitive hits for the day before I even get out of bed.

Pay attention to the information you're receiving. You are receiving information all the time, now it's time to witness it. Observe what you're getting and see if you can create a habit of following through. Notice what arrives, follow through on as much of it as you can, and see what happens.

I have a "five second rule." If a thought comes into my mind, I share it or I act on it. If you let it pass, it's gone, it's in the past. When I teach psychic mediumship, I like to say:

"No one wants to hear a psychic say, 'I was just thinking that,' after they say something."

Any thoughts you get, write them down. Any ideas, write them down. If you get mental pictures, images, or little mini movies, notice how they relate to your personal experience or someone else's. Notice feelings in relation to your environment or the people around you. Notice any out of the ordinary smells, tastes, or anything you may "hear." Ask yourself: Is this something I should follow through on? Is this guidance for me or for someone else?

Then see if you can implement a practice of acting on that information.

Set the intention that you are going to follow your intuition. You're going to go for it. You're going to trust yourself. You are doing this for you. This is your first step in living an intuitive life, in living your best life.

Write it down. Pay attention. What thoughts are coming through? Jot them down. You will start noticing more. You will start seeing more. You will begin to feel yourself entering a flow with life. You'll step into the stream of information available to us at all times.

Get curious. Start asking yourself: "Was that my intuition?"

Was that a message from the Universe, the Universal Field, or the All That Is?

The Universe will (and always has) conspire to help you. You will notice synchronicities more. You will see coincidences more. You will begin seeing repeating numbers on clocks, billboards, and license plates. People will say exactly what you need to hear at exactly the right moment. Your goosebumps may start or increase. You will begin noticing breadcrumbs placed along your path. You will feel the threads that connect you to everything and everyone. You will feel supported by the Universe.

Set your intention now to pay attention, to notice, to follow, to track. Write down what comes, and see which intuitive hits open doors for you or help you in some way.

This is the fun part. This is when you begin to see the magic of life unfolding before your eyes. Get excited. Start listening to your intuition. Trust yourself.

Set the intention. Pay attention. And enjoy the process.

Be ready to see how the Universe conspires to help you.

Building Your Foundation

Strengthening Your Energetic Body

Strengthening our energetic state and field starts with our body. Our body is the vehicle for our soul, the physical manifestation we chose to live this life in, and the vehicle through which consciousness experiences itself. I heard **Gregg Braden** say this recently: *"Consciousness communicates with itself through the things that it creates. Consciousness informs itself through its creation."* We are a part of that creation.

We receive information with and through our body through our physical senses. So, what better place to start than with our bodies? There is so much within our physical landscape, and in what we feed our body and mind, that affects our energetic system and vice versa.

Let us begin with diet. And when I say diet, I don't just mean food. Yes, food is a part of the whole, but not the entirety. Our diet is everything we take in from food to media content, and everything in between. All of these things either raise or lower our vibration or frequency state. We are energetic beings, and we have a vibrational frequency component; we're not just material or physical, as we've been told. As a matter of fact, we aren't really material in nature. We feel physical that is our lived experience until we discover that we're actually not.

We are a mental reality. "The All is Mind; the universe is mental." **The Kybalion** which discusses the seven Hermetic Principles. One of the old Hermetic masters wrote: *"He who grasps the truth of the mental nature of the universe is well advanced on the path of mastery."*

Our reality, matter, energy, the material universe that engages our physical senses is Spirit. We have tried to define it in many ways and with many names. Religion calls it God. Spirituality calls it the Universe, Universal Consciousness, or Divine Energy. Spirit is ineffable: a larger consciousness mind that is the source of all existence. A universal living mind, Creator and all of creation being a mental creation of the All.

Simply knowing this truth gives you a key to unlocking your psychic intuitive nature, and your awareness of energy, matter, power, and mastery of mind.

With this understanding, we see that everything is in motion, nothing is at rest, and everything vibrates. This is verified by science repeatedly. From the table in front of you, to the walls, to you and Spirit, everything is vibration. Spirit is at the top of the vibrational scale and that table at the lower end as we see it today.

The reason we can't "see" the other realms that are always around us is because they are vibrating at a higher rate of speed and out of our normal awareness. But by increasing our vibration and opening to our psychic abilities, we can reach states where we not only see, but can interact with Spirit and with the multidimensional field we are a part of.

When we are in low vibrational states, our intuitive dial turns down. Low emotional states such as fear, anxiety, depression, and judgment lower our vibration and keep our intuition at bay. Higher vibrational states such as love, joy, happiness, kindness, gratitude, and a positive outlook turn up the dial on our intuition.

When we are functioning at the top of the vibrational scale, we are in alignment with our higher states of being. From there, we can be in alignment with our natural flow state experiencing better health, happiness, and peace of mind. Not to mention being in alignment with our soul's path and a beautiful organic unfoldment of life.

You are able to reach this natural unfolding of life laid before you because you become a magnet for what is in alignment with you, based on your vibrational state of being. You attract what you are. The Law of Attraction states that our thoughts, feelings, and intentions influence our reality by attracting similar energies. Therefore, if you are in a higher vibrational state, you will attract higher vibrational experiences and vice versa.

That's not to say we will be void of difficulty. Lessons happen. It simply means that where your attention goes, energy flows. What you focus on, you manifest more of in your life.

There are many ways we can ensure we are functioning at a high vibrational state supporting and increasing our intuitive capabilities. Let's begin with the basics.

Clean, filtered, chemical-free, or naturally sourced drinking water; coconut water; and other healthy options like herbal tea benefit both our physical and energetic bodies. We are lucky here on Vashon that our city water is free of fluoride. Fluoride, for example, can inhibit pineal gland function and, in some cases, calcify it.

The pineal gland often referred to as the third eye, is considered a center of spiritual perception and insight, and connects us to Source Consciousness at the 7th chakra. Pineal activation can lead to increased intuition and spiritual awakening.

Things that protect and enhance the pineal gland include:

- Sleeping in a dark bedroom to support melatonin production
- Wearing blue light glasses during screen time (blue light can suppress melatonin)
- Receiving the sun's rays indirectly through the eyes (not staring directly at the sun)
- Consuming an antioxidant-rich, plant-based diet
- Avoiding fluoride and processed calcium
- Being informed about current medication and vaccine side effects
- Wearing the Alveda Lifewave patch at night (see "Shop My Favorites" on my website)
- Meditation
- Breathwork
- Kundalini activation

Alcohol and caffeine inhibit intuition. I've known highly psychic individuals who use alcohol to turn off their constant stream of information. Limiting, or avoiding, alcohol and caffeinated drinks like coffee allows your mental capacities to stay focused and alert. The cleaner and clearer you are, the higher your vibe.

At least, this is the case for me. I have decaf coffee at times living here in Pacific Northwest coffee culture but I've stopped on occasion (once for 10 years) and felt noticeably brighter. There are many herbal alternatives to fill the void, some with added adaptogens. And if I have a client, having a drink is a hard no. I've reached a point in my life where I rarely drink at all and being sensitive, it never took much for me anyway.

For years I have heard how beneficial a vegetarian diet is. I was vegetarian briefly in my 20s (bacon broke me!). And now, I've been vegetarian for over 15 years. For me, the switch came after a week-long visit to my hometown in Cambridge, MD. I'd been visiting my dad and felt terrible upon returning home, and I didn't know why.

The following week, I had a dream. In that dream, a woman approached me and said I was to become vegetarian. After that dream, I simply didn't crave meat anymore. It benefited me physically as well - at my next yearly checkup, my blood work came back great. No more high cholesterol.

I'm sharing this because everyone is different and our bodies need different diets depending on our individual constitutions. This is for you to intuitively decide for yourself. Looking back over the years, I see that I had a natural progression with food and sourcing:

- A regular American diet
- Then label-reading

- Then buying healthier options and organic foods
- Then sourcing meat from local farms (farm-to-table)
- Then growing my own vegetables and keeping my own fowl
- Then eventually removing meat products

It's been a step-by-step opening to a healthier relationship with food, animals, and the Earth.

Our relationship with food impacts our environment. We have only to look at documentaries on soil, farming, and animal husbandry to become aware. Eliminating chemicals as best we can from our food, water, air, and Earth is ideal. Being aware of different farming practices, as well as what we put on our yards, impacts soil, water supply, the planet, and us.

Fruits and vegetables grown in clean soil, and animals raised consciously, are higher in vibration. I also believe that as your frequency rises, you naturally begin to make dietary changes for yourself as a consequence of your evolution.

As you evolve, you'll notice that you are led to yoga, meditation, and spending time in nature. Yoga may begin as a passing thought, a different thing to try at the gym. For me, yoga was the first exercise I was intuitively drawn to that made me want to eat better afterward. It centers, grounds, and brings balance.

Yoga was one of the gateways that led me to meditation and more. Meditation not only calms the mind, but brings peace, non-reactivity, and a sense of calm in any given situation.

Getting in touch with your breath also brings you into balance and equanimity. It grounds you, brings you into your inner world, increases your energy and the flow of energy throughout your body, activates your kundalini life-force energy, and strengthens your energetic field and body.

Everything works together to bring us into wholeness:

- The seen: our physical, material body
- And the unseen: our energetic body

Our aura, our central channel (hara and sushumna), and our chakras. These systems inside and out are important for us to be aware of, and what we bring into our body affects all of them. Not just our physical systems, but our energetic systems as well.

Having awareness of what strengthens our physical and energetic systems can go a long way in helping us intuitively. But we also need to look at what we're ingesting from our external environment.

What kind of TV are we watching?

What kind of movies?

What are we digesting while we scroll on our phones?

Are we watching too much news?

All of these things affect what we magnetize to ourselves. What we see and ingest, we become. Who you hang around with, what you watch - your life is like an algorithm. Whatever you put your attention on, you attract and get more of. Where attention goes, energy flows.

I heard recently in a reel my oldest son sent me that just 15 minutes of the news causes stress. I agree. It's an epidemic, and it keeps getting worse. It's not like it was in the 80s and 90s when I was younger.

Personally, I unplugged in 2020. It was about the stress. I could feel my energy changing and my limbic system (fight, flight, freeze) being activated as I watched and listened. I also noticed when I traveled during lockdown and beyond that the news stations in restaurants where I'd pick up to go food were spinning different narratives in each place I visited, with key, inciting language woven into the dialogue. Stirring the pot and playing to people's emotions. I wanted no part of it divisive or otherwise.

How much stress do you have in your life? Are you taking steps to lessen that stress?

Many of us have so much going on that we're rarely in our parasympathetic nervous system (rest and restore) and are functioning mainly from our sympathetic nervous system (fight or flight). That wears us down. It taxes our adrenals, making us feel tired and leaving us with little to no energy.

Then we can get into a cycle of relying on tea, coffee, energy drinks, and sports drinks to pull us out of that fatigue. Instead of relying on "fake energy," getting enough sleep, taking time to rest and relax, stepping away from stressful people and situations, having a yoga and meditation practice, and going on walks in nature can bring us back into balance.

Sleep is very important for our intuitive abilities. Sleep enhances intuition. If I don't get enough sleep, I don't have good dream recall or I don't remember my dreams at all. Not only do we heal and process in our sleep, but our dream time is a key area for intuiting vital information about and for our lives.

It's one of the ways Spirit can give us messages, our deceased loved ones can interact with us, and we can receive precognitive guidance. And when we are well rested, our brains function better. That gives us the ability to process information more clearly and gain clarity, which leads to clearer intuition. I know if I don't get enough sleep, my brain goes offline. Sleep!

Taking the time to find that balance within is what strengthens our energetic system, not only our physical, mental, and emotional bodies, but our energetic bodies as well. Having all of these systems functioning harmoniously really helps us be in tune with, and have full access to, intuition.

When we are balanced, we can receive more, know more; and do so in a deeply grounded way.

Pulling away from stress, getting a good night's sleep, and eating and drinking nourishing things, these are all practices that help raise our vibration, strengthen our energetic system, and increase our intuitive potential.

Grounding

Grounding plays an important role in strengthening our energetic fields. It's one of the first things we learn in energy work, and it takes practice to build our energy body's strength to stay in a grounded state. Our energy fields build strength and resilience just like our physical bodies.

Just as when we want to step into our own personal empowerment, one of the first things we often do is strengthen our physical body, the same goes for our energy body. This is one of the first things I did in my late 30s when I was in a process of taking my power back: I hit the gym. Later, I noticed how common this response was when I saw the same progression in others. I see a similar pattern in taking our energetic power back as well.

Part of feeling whole, centered, and grounded in who we are is getting grounded within ourselves.

Grounding is being fully, energetically, and spiritually in your body - embodied and connected to the earth. It is feet firmly planted on the ground, awareness of our physical body, and bringing our spirit selves fully into it. It is bringing our energy body - which often spends a lot of time outside of our body - back into our center - Embodied.

So why does our spirit spend so much time outside of our body? Because we can be very analytical. We spend a lot of time in our heads (left brain), always thinking. When we're stuck in our mind, we're out of our body out of presence. We're programmed in our society to always be on the go, always busy, always striving, always doing. It's a very masculine way of being.

The masculine, or yang energy, is action-oriented, direct, penetrating. The divine feminine is yin energy intuition, creativity, surrendering to the flow of life.

Being stuck in our heads ironically often leaves us unaware of and detached from our physical body. We need to bring our energy back into our body to find balance to find our center, to be fully within and embodied.

It feels very different to be out of the body than to be in the body. Feeling ungrounded can show up as feeling off balance, dizzy, dissociated, tripping over things, being clumsy, spacing out, daydreaming, or feeling like you're "in your head."

When you're feeling grounded, you may feel connected to the earth, notice tingling on your skin, or feel a weighted, heavier sensation. I feel it as a heavy sensation as my inner Spirit self-embodies, a coming together into presence and physical awareness. It is a very physical experience for me, feeling my body "come alive" again.

It takes energetic muscles to stay grounded. If you're not used to being in a grounded state, you'll likely find yourself going in and out often and needing to repeatedly bring yourself back in consciously.

I'm seeing more and more that people are going through energetic upgrades. When you get an energetic upgrade, it's a vibratory upgrade to your energetic system, and it can take a minute for your physical body to catch up. Sometimes there's no physical reaction, but other times it can feel quite uncomfortable in the body.

You may feel like your physical body isn't a comfortable space feeling anxious or uneasy in your own skin. When I experience this, I take a personal time out to breathe or take an Epsom salts bath or both. It always does the trick, and I feel my nervous system regulate almost immediately, accompanied by a sigh of relief.

Our energetics are always ahead of our physical. That's why you can psychically see something before it happens. Energy precedes physical time and space as we see it.

That's why, when you sign up for a workshop or healing session, the healing often begins before you even get there. It's why intuitions come moments beforehand. It's why I receive information about a client well before their scheduled time.

Energy is ahead of our linear concept of time, that's why you hear "time is an illusion." Time is a man-made construct. There really is no time or space in the way we experience it in this 3rd dimensional field of awareness. We can go backward or forward in time and space with ease because it's all right here, right now.

During a session with clients, I'm working in this quantum field. It's timeless. I can access a past life or Spirit just as easily as I can access you in the present moment.

I also see that my clients are bringing in more light. We are all upleveling with this shift in our own ways and have access to more cosmic light. We each have our own trajectory and life path and our own way of getting there, but some are gaining access to diamond white light, gold light. Some are connecting to the crystalline earth grid, and we are being asked by the Earth if we'd like to blend with her like we blend with Spirit in mediumship, becoming one with the Earth.

This is a beautiful experience and awakens an awareness of being part of the Earth herself.

I'm also seeing people beginning the process of, or becoming, Soul Embodied. Soul Embodiment is when our Soul self takes up full-time residence in our physical body and becomes integrated into the self. The small "s" self is who we identify as in this life (the avatar, so to speak), and the big "S" Self is our Soul Self (or Spirit, or Higher Self, as it has been called).

When we are taught to meditate, the big "S" Self is often seen as the observer outside the body. As your Soul integrates, this big "S" Self takes up residence within the body. From form to formlessness becoming Soul-led. When the Soul takes over, there is no longer a "middle man." Life flows from Source to you.

This state is also more feminine in nature - intuition based, living in a flow state. It can feel like a state of unknowing, since life becomes a process of unfolding rather than being goal oriented. Very different from the constant "knowingness" we had from relying on a planned future in the past.

At first, the Soul self can be in and out of the body, negotiating with the Ego self. This can happen naturally for those who are ready during this shift. They've moved past their predestined karmic lessons and are now stepping into Soul work, where the past is in the past period. It's a paradigm shift, a new reality or timeline altogether.

You feel connected to the All That Is; your old job or old way of doing things no longer feels in alignment; people fade from your life and new ones step forward. You become a whole new you with a different trajectory in life. You are in direct connection with Source Consciousness.

This looks like following your intuition, following your ideas and insights, living in synchronicity, surrendering to flow, knowing all is in divine alignment and you may begin attracting Soul partnerships and friendships instead of karmic relationships.

Because the Ego self wants to remain in control and keep the human you safe, this process can be challenging. You may have heard of people going through an ego death because of a spiritual awakening or a psychedelic experience; a similar experience as a comparison, but different because Soul embodiment doesn't always follow. In the earlier example, the ego releases, giving way to more Soul access and a reconfiguring of the self.

During the process of Soul Embodiment, negotiations with the ego can be disorienting or involve mental disorganization and fear, and may cause an energetic fracturing (a mental split) in the aura or biofield leaving you wondering if you are losing your mind as the ego fights to stay in charge.

This can be seen in spontaneous spiritual awakenings and sudden awakenings due to psychedelic experiences. This happens because these experiences can open the doorway to Consciousness abruptly, and people may not be prepared for that awakening to a new perspective, or reality, or for the ability to hold both this reality and the other sides.

If you are experiencing this, it's important to stop fighting it, release fear, and find a space of peaceful acceptance within yourself. Seek help from an informed therapist and energy worker. When integrated, you can hold both sides in a balanced, neutral way, and the fear dissolves.

In a state of allowing, you surrender into observing and learning this new you, your new normal as it naturally unfolds, settles, and integrates.

This experience can be a very peaceful transition if you are able to surrender to the process, stay grounded within yourself, and have full faith in the processes of life; letting go of outcome, striving, or searching.

There are ecstatic states of awakening - feeling joy and bliss and seeing the oneness and beauty of life. And there is a less commonly discussed empty state. This is a state of stillness, "no-thing-ness," where you may feel lost, uninterested in doing anything, lying around wondering if you were better off not knowing - before awakening. This is also a state of awakening.

When we become Soul Embodied, functioning fully from our Soul aspect, we allow Soul to lead the way - to speak through us and act through us. We become Soul-led instead of ego-led or ego-driven. We live in a state of peace, experiencing oneness with the All, fully aware that we are a fractal of Source Consciousness and receiving a constant flow of intel - intuition from the river of Consciousness, experiencing a constant stream of synchronicities.

A flow state where everything seems divinely orchestrated - because it is - where you have everything you need at any given moment; completely guided and supported by Source. Fully grounded in yourself, connected to the cosmos, and fully connected to and grounded into the Earth.

When you are actively connecting to the Earth, you are grounding and grounded. You're fully engaged and present. You have improved focus and clarity of thought and therefore clearer action. You become unshakable. You are better in touch with your intuition, balanced, and centered. You "feel" in your body; firmly planted, solid, and you have a sense of strength about you.

Bringing yourself down into your body is beneficial and important not only for your state of presence, but also because, when you are grounded, you manage life and your emotional states with more ease. You are less likely to take on others' energies and emotions, and you know your boundaries in space and time in any given moment or situation.

If you experience any type of difficulty whether from a person, a stressful situation, or an event, the first thing I recommend is to ground. This gives you a calm and balanced way of dealing with and navigating whatever comes your way.

There are different ways you can get grounded.

- Touch your body, shoulders, arms, and legs with firm hands to come into present awareness.
- Squeeze your feet, one at a time.
- Have some nourishing food.
- Take your shoes off and place your bare feet on the ground stand on the earth.
- Bend your knees a few times; activating your thighs brings you back into your legs.
- Go out into nature, allowing the negative ions to ground you.

- Detach from your devices and TV and take a moment to be present with yourself.
- Turn on some music and move or dance to get into your body.
- Run, jog, meditate, do yoga, go for a hike or a bike ride, and feel the air on your skin, draw your attention to your physicality.
- Get a massage.

These are all ways to get in touch with your body and become grounded and embodied.

It's about taking steps to come out of your head and return to your body, your center, your heart. When you come into your heart center, this also grounds your energy back down into your body, and back into presence.

To do this, you can bring your awareness to your heart center - visually imagine sinking into your heart. Dropping your chin slightly, or placing your hand on your heart, helps you find your center and become embodied.

There are benefits to harmonizing the brain and the heart. This is called heart mind coherence. There are many benefits beyond grounding: accessing the subconscious, increased cognitive learning and memory, and deepened intuition.

HeartMath Institute recommends a short, three-minute heart coherence meditation. It uses controlled breathing, focused attention, and positive emotion to create harmony between the heart and brain. It is scientifically shown to strengthen the immune system, balance the nervous system, and reduce stress, especially in challenging times. It is the science-based practice of synchronizing your heart and your brain.

"This alignment balances your nervous system and creates coherence between your heart, mind, and emotions, which is key to clearing stress and unlocking your higher capacities," says **HeartMath Institute.**

1. Heart-focused breathing

Place your hand on your chest, shifting your attention to the area of your heart. Imagine your breath flowing in and out of this area, breathing a little slower and deeper than usual. A comfortable rhythm is inhaling for five seconds and exhaling for five seconds.

2. Activate a regenerative feeling

While continuing heart-focused breathing, sincerely attempt to experience a feeling of gratitude. Recall a time in your life when you felt appreciation, care, or love for someone or something. This positive emotion helps create a coherent heart rhythm pattern.

3. Add music (optional)

Use an instrumental song that invokes a sense of love or caring for about three minutes.

We are born into this physical planet, into these physical bodies, to live a physical existence. Although we can awaken to other states of being through meditation or ecstatic bliss, we incarnated into physical form to remember that we are eternal beings through this physical experience.

We are Spirit having a physical experience. We are not our bodies or our minds, even though we incarnated for this earthly journey. We will again leave these physical selves, but while we are here in the now, we are meant to embody ourselves.

We have the ability to go to deep spiritual places by going within, and we can be more connected to Source, Spirit, Consciousness.

Through embodiment, pulling ourselves back into center, we experience presence in the present moment. Moment by moment.

When we are presently grounded, we hear, listen, and feel our way through life far better than if we were outside of our body.

So, let's get physically grounded, energetically grounded, Soul Embodied - Spirit within, Soul-led.

Grounded. Present. Connected. Aware. Intuitively led.

Exercises We Can Do to Get Grounded

- Imagine your feet firmly planted on the ground.
- Get your bare feet on the earth.
- Squeeze your feet with your hands.
- With your mental awareness, go up your body joint by joint from your feet to the top of your head to bring yourself into present awareness.
- Find your center by connecting to your heart center. Imagine the center of the center of the center of your internal being.
- When you are grounded in your body, you are centered, balanced, present in the moment, make better decisions, and you can hear, see, feel, and receive your intuition with clarity.

Daily Guided Grounding Meditation

- Standing in a tall, upright position, knees slightly bent, place your left hand on your lower abdomen and your right hand on your heart. Dip your chin slightly toward your chest. Feel into your feet.

- Imagine a grounding cord going down into the center of the Earth. Wrap that cord around a rock in the molten core at the center of the Earth. Feel the weight of gravity upon your head and shoulders as you sink into the ground beneath you.

- Imagine now that you're pulling Earth energy up into your body through this cord. As you inhale, the energy rises up to the top of your head, and as you exhale, this energy flows back down to your feet.

- Feel the sensation of your energetic body inside your physical body feeling the weight of gravity all around you: from the top of your head, your shoulders, and the tension in your thighs. Use your imagination to feel your body all the way down into your feet.

Running Energy

What is running energy?

Running energy is a fundamental exercise in the energy work system. This technique is used to increase energy flow, clear blockages, and promote balance in the human energy field (aura). The primary goal is to consciously move energy also referred to as ki, chi, prana, or universal life force through the body's central energy channel and the chakras.

The basic process generally involves grounding, centering, bringing in universal energy, and circulating that energy.

By running energy, individuals can identify and release areas of stagnation or "blocked energy" and charge depleted areas. This energy is moved consciously through the body's major energy centers (chakras) and the central channel (sushumna), promoting fluid and balanced movement.

This is the process known as "running energy." You draw energy in from above the head (the universal field) and from below the feet (the Earth field). The exercise typically begins by establishing a strong connection to the Earth via grounding and to the universal energy field by connecting above. This helps create a stable foundation for the energy pathway.

Running energy helps you enhance your ability to perceive energy, maintain a clear and flowing energy field, and is a practical tool for self-care. It allows you to clear your own field and promotes self-awareness. It supports physical, emotional, mental, and spiritual health.

By running energy, you remove things from your energy system that would be considered unhealthy, such as emotional and energetic blocks, and energy you've picked up from other people, places, and things.

You might be asking, how do I feel and sense energy?

You can learn to feel and sense energy by practicing awareness of your body and using a simple exercise such as rubbing your hands together and moving them slowly apart and closer together to feel a tingling or magnetic sensation between your palms. Focusing on physical sensations like tingling, heat, or pressure and practicing mindfulness and meditation can help you tune into subtle energy.

Learning to sense your own internal energy as well as energy from people and nature is a skill that develops with regular practice.

Exercise to Feel Energy in Your Hands

1. Rub your hands together for about 30 seconds to build friction.
2. Hold your hands out in front of you with your fingers relaxed.
3. Slowly bring your palms closer to one another without touching.
4. Focus on the space between your palms and notice any sensations like tingling, heat, pressure, or a magnetic pull.
5. Experiment by pulling and pushing your hands together and apart to feel the energy between your palms.
6. Try placing your hands near different parts of your body, like your head or knees, to see if you can sense energy there.
7. You can also practice this with a partner by placing your palms facing your partner's palms (without touching) and see if you can feel the energy between your hands.

When I'm working with clients, this is the energy that I am channeling through my energy system to them. I am a conduit for the energy to facilitate healing and awaken the client's natural healing capabilities, and I can navigate it.

You can also train this energy to travel through your body and move through your energetic system removing blocks in the body, chakras, and clearing negative and stagnant energies that keep you stuck.

Clearing energy is important for improving mental and emotional well-being, reducing stress, creating mental clarity, and being able to release and heal our emotional wounds. It benefits you in other ways as well, including increased vitality, better sleep, and improved physical health, because it balances and restores the body's natural energy field.

By releasing negative and stagnant energy, you come into equanimity and become more balanced, able to hold a state of inner harmony, and become more receptive. When we have a clear energetic system and a nice, strong, straight central channel (sushumna), we become more aligned with our life's purpose as well.

Running Energy Exercise

1. Standing with a tall spine, feet planted hip-width apart, place your left hand on your lower abdomen and your right hand on your heart. Take a deep breath and bring your energy body into your physical body.

2. Send your grounding cord down into the center of the Earth, feeling your body become heavier as you sense gravity upon your head, shoulders, body, and the tension in your thighs.

3. Imagine energy coming up through this grounding cord into your physical body as you inhale.

4. Bring this energy up through the 1st chakra at the base of your body or perineum, into your central channel, an energetic channel that travels up through the center of your body in front of your spine.

5. On your next inhale, bring this energy up into your 2nd chakra, right below your navel.

6. On your next inhale, bring the energy up into your 3rd chakra right below your rib cage at your solar plexus or upper stomach.

7. Once again, inhale the energy up, this time into your heart, the 4th chakra.

8. On the next inhale, rise this energy up into your throat, the 5th chakra.

9. Continuing, on the next inhale bring that energy up into your 6th chakra at your forehead, between your eyebrows.

10. Finally, breathe that energy up to the top of your head and out the crown.

11. On your next inhale, bring that energy from the bottoms of your feet all the way to the top of your head. On your exhale, send the energy back down from the top of your head to your feet.

12. Continue breathing the energy in and sending it back down for several minutes.

The Aura

The aura, or human energy field biofield, as scientists like to call it, is an energetic field of energy that surrounds the body. It is a field of colored light that emanates from a living being, plant, or object. The auric field has seven layers, each one with a different function, structure, and level of vibration.

This field reflects an individual's inner state, personality, emotions, and overall well-being. The first three layers relate to the physical, etheric, and emotional levels, and the next four correspond to the spiritual self. Each layer interacts with the others. Different colors are associated with specific qualities and emotional states, such as red for passion, green for healing, and indigo for intuition.

The aura also reflects the chakras, which are our energy centers in the body. This field of energy is comprised of seven layers, each layer lying on top of the next until it reaches the outer golden edge of the 7th layer of the field. Hence one of the names for our field: "the golden egg." Imbalances in any one of these layers can manifest as physical, emotional, or mental issues, and can be cleared through energy healing to promote overall well-being.

The odd layers of the field are structured, and the even layers of the field are unstructured, meaning they are cloud-like. The fifth layer of the field is unique, as it is the divine grid of our field or divine template. There is also a divine grid that we can energetically interact with in the greater universal field. During energy sessions, this field can be dropped down and worked on in correspondence with the fifth layer of our own auric field.

Barbara Brennan states that it is "a multidimensional energetic structure of reality which includes the physical body, the human energy field, and the spiritual dimensions of the Hara (intention) and the core star (divine spark). This grid, sometimes called the four dimensions of humankind, serves as an energetic map for understanding and transforming one's health and spiritual journey."

For clarity:

- The hara is the level of intention and purpose, which includes the Hara line and tan tien (power center), a central energy point in the body. The hara is also a concept in Japanese traditions, referring to the body's core energy center in the abdomen, about 2 inches below the navel.
- The sushumna is the central energy channel along the energetic spine in yogic traditions.

- They are different, but both relate to the flow of life force energy.
- The core star is our divine spark or essence, a brilliantly radiant soul spark of our being that resides within every person.

The human energy field is a multilayered, egg-shaped field with seven auric layers, each corresponding to a different aspect of a person's being - each person having a unique aura structure – and it is always in flux. The layers are:

- The etheric body: the physical body/sensory layer
- The emotional body: our feelings layer
- The mental body: our thought layer
- The astral body: a bridge between the physical world and higher spiritual realms
- The etheric template: higher will and blueprint
- The celestial body: spiritual connection and consciousness
- The causal body: our divine connection

Do You Have a Desire to See the Aura?

One of the easiest ways to see an aura is to place a person or object in front of a white wall and softly gaze at them. Another way to see an aura is by looking at trees against the backdrop of a clear blue sky. The aura of a tree in summertime is green, and during the winter months, the aura of the trees often appears more reddish. Gazing at the tops of trees is a fun way to learn how to see auras and is often one of the first ways people notice energy around living things.

Another fun way to practice seeing auras is to allow your gaze to soften while you look at a person on a video call. You may start to see a glow around their body, often at the top of, or around, their head.

As you lift your vibration through various means including meditation, breathwork, and the exercises I've shared earlier, you may start to see energy fields, often beginning with a slight glow around people. Like a bubble, the aura can extend outward six-plus feet. Older souls and people who have sight often have very large fields.

We can also bring our fields in if we need tighter boundaries such as on an airplane. We're all interacting with and within each other's fields all the time, sending information back and forth and energetically sensing whether a person, place, or thing is okay for us or not. It is a receiving field, and it is also gathering information from our surroundings. Before we interact with our eyes or our voice, our energy fields are already surveying our environment.

An example of sensing energetically: when you suddenly look up and notice someone is looking at you. This happens because your energy felt that someone else's energy was tapping (energetically touching) into yours. This is why sometimes a look from someone can feel slimy, or you can actually feel someone's hate coming at you. Energetically they are indeed sending you those emotions from their field to yours.

The saying "sticks and stones can break my bones but words can never hurt me" seems all well and good, but we all know that's not true. And the same goes for energy. People send emotions of all kinds, daggers from their eyes, projections, and more. You name it, it's possible. And when you know, you know.

So next time you think of giving someone a dirty look, think about what you are actually doing. This is a good time to mention: the person with the most information about the impact they are actually causing holds the responsibility in any given situation. Do you want to be responsible for causing energetic harm?

The Seven Layers of the Auric Field

1st Layer (Physical/Etheric): The most physical layer, closest to the body, associated with physical sensations.

2nd Layer (Emotional/Astral): Holds emotions and feelings and can be influenced by unprocessed emotional information from daily life.

3rd Layer (Mental): Corresponds to thoughts, intellect, and conscious perception.

4th Layer (Astral): Connects to the heart chakra and is related to love, compassion, spiritual connection, and out-of-body experiences.

5th Layer (Etheric Template): The blueprint for the physical body and represents the will and intention of the spiritual self.

6th Layer (Celestial): Associated with clairvoyance and divine love; the realm of the Higher Self.

7th Layer (Causal/Spiritual): The highest layer the spiritual body and the connection to universal consciousness.

Creating an Energetic Bubble of Protection

It's important to have a practice of energetic protection when you need it.

To create an energy bubble of protection, take a deep breath to center yourself and close your eyes to relax, if that feels comfortable. Visualize a bubble of white or golden light surrounding your body or choose a color that feels right to you. You can strengthen the bubble by imagining a reflective surface, like a mirror, on the outside to bounce negative energy away from you. I like to imagine a field that allows love in and keeps negativity out.

Step-by-step guide:

1. Take a few slow, deep breaths to relax and release any tension.
2. Close your eyes and imagine a shimmering bubble of light forming around you, extending 1–6 feet in every direction.
3. Select a color that resonates with you for your bubble, white for purity, blue for tranquility, or golden light for power and protection.
4. Strengthen the bubble:
   - Use affirmations: Repeat positive affirmations like, "I am safe and protected."
   - Breathe energy in: As you inhale, visualize positive energy flowing into the bubble. As you exhale, see that energy expanding and filling the bubble to make it stronger.
   - Add a reflective layer: Imagine the outside of the bubble covered in a reflective material, like tiny crystals or mirrors, so any negative energy bounces off instead of coming through.

5. Focus on your intention for the bubble to be a shield that filters out negativity and allows in only positive energy.

6. Practice this regularly such as each morning to create a sense of calm, peace, and strength.

Energetic Aura Clearing Exercises

• Smudge with sage, Palo Santo, or a local cleansing herb. You can also create a sage spray with essential oils and water to use where smoke isn't allowed (I keep one in my purse). Smudge or spray yourself. This also works well for your surroundings. Don't forget your car, it needs a good energetic cleaning occasionally too.

• While you are in the shower, as the water washes over you, imagine a shower of white light cleansing and clearing your aura.

• Use a brushing motion with your hands over your body as if you are brushing dust off your arms, legs, and torso. Do this with the intention of brushing off unwanted energies.

• Ask Archangel Michael: *"Please remove everything that does not belong to me and is not for my highest and best good."*

• Imagine you are standing in a hoop of light. Pull this hoop of light up your entire body, imagining it as a net of light gathering everything that doesn't belong to you, then surrender it to a higher power above to be transmuted into love.

- Take an Epsom salt and baking soda bath, 1 cup of each (you can add essential oils if desired).
- Go for a swim in salt water.
- Get out into nature, take a walk in the woods or forest.
- Stand in the wind and imagine the wind is blowing out and clearing your aura.

The Chakras

The word chakra originates from Hindu and Buddhist tantric traditions and translates to wheel of light, or simply "wheel" in Sanskrit. This refers to the spinning wheels of life-energy that flow through the body's subtle energy system. Barbara Brennan's work detailed in her books *Hands of Light* and *Light Emerging* popularized the seven major chakra model, with each chakra corresponding to specific physical, emotional, mental, and spiritual functions.

There are seven major energy centers (chakras) in the body. While there are more, we will focus on the well-known physical seven. They begin at the perineum with the 1st chakra and continue up the energetic spine, the central channel - sushumna to the top of the head, the 7th chakra.

Chakras are shaped like cones, with the point of the cone directed inward toward the central channel, and the open side facing outward, forward for the front chakras and backward for the rear chakras. Picture a pointed ice cream cone: the point touches the spine, and the open end faces outward into the space in front or behind you.

Chakras take in and process energy from the Universal Energy Field, distributing it to the physical body and the different layers of the aura. They are crucial for sustaining physical, emotional, and spiritual wellbeing. Each chakra corresponds to a layer in the energetic field. The 1st chakra points downward, the next five face the front and back of the body, and the 7th points upward.

At each chakra point there is a cluster of nerve endings - nerve plexuses that correspond to that area of the body. Each chakra relates to the organs, psychic gifts, and endocrine glands of that particular region.

When a chakra is unbalanced, it is pointing to issues in the physical body or in your life. For example, an unbalanced root chakra may correlate to fear or insecurity. Practices such as meditation, yoga, Reiki, and other forms of energy work help realign the chakras and restore harmony. Free-flowing life force energy is vital for mental, physical, and spiritual health.

The Seven Major Chakras

1. Root Chakra (Muladhara) : "I Am"

Location: Located at the base of the spine, the root chakra is associated with safety, security, grounding, money, and stability.

Color: Red

When unbalanced: You may feel fearful, anxious, unstable, or experience issues with the lower back, colon, or bladder.

Mantra: Lam

2. Sacral Chakra (Svadhisthana) :"I Feel"

Location: Located below the navel, this chakra governs creativity, emotions, sexuality, pleasure, and self-worth.

Color: Orange

When unbalanced: You may experience emotional swings, addictive tendencies, creative blocks, or sexual imbalance.

Mantra: Vam

3. Solar Plexus Chakra (Manipura): "I Do"

Location: Found in the upper stomach area, this chakra aligns with personal power, confidence, boundaries, and self-esteem.

Color: Yellow

When unbalanced: Symptoms may include anger, low confidence, control issues, or digestive troubles.

Mantra: Ram

4. Heart Chakra (Anahata) : "I Love"

Location: Located at the center of the chest, the heart chakra governs love, compassion, trust, forgiveness, and clairsentience.

Color: Green

When unbalanced: You may experience jealousy, grief, anger, lack of boundaries, or heart palpitations.

Mantra: Yam

5. Throat Chakra (Vishuddha): "I Speak"

Location: Located at the throat, this chakra rules communication, truth, self-expression, and authenticity. It connects to clairaudience, clairgustance, and clairalience.

Color: Blue

When unbalanced: You may struggle to express yourself or experience thyroid issues, headaches, or throat discomfort.

Mantra: Ham

6. Third Eye Chakra (Ajna): "I See"

Location: Found between the eyebrows, this chakra governs intuition, inner wisdom, psychic sight, and spiritual insight.

Color: Indigo

When unbalanced: Symptoms may include doubting intuition, headaches, judgmental thinking, or blurry vision.

Mantra: Sham

7. Crown Chakra (Sahasrara): "I Understand"

Location: Located at the top of the head, the crown chakra represents spiritual connection, enlightenment, inner knowing, and purpose.

Color: Violet or White

When unbalanced: You may feel disconnected, spiritually blocked, apathetic, or depressed.

Mantra: Om

Cording and the Chakras

Cording refers to the subtle energetic connections we form with people. This can happen naturally in relationships or when someone tries to influence or control us. A healthy cord looks like a gentle energetic handshake. For example, a balanced friendship of give and take, a partnership based on equality, and the mother-child cord present from birth are representations of healthy cording - minus control dynamics.

A power over cord, however, looks like a hand reaching in and grabbing someone's chakra. These cords can form when someone wants to influence your emotions, your decisions, or even your thoughts. A person trying to control your thinking may cord your mind or implant a thought form; anything from a persistent belief to an internalized phrase like, "You can't live without me."

Cords can come from this life or past lives. Relationship cords are the most common. A simple cord-cutting process can disconnect the bond.

One time a client wanted to cut their energetic cord with their mother. After the session, she checked her phone and saw a text from her mother saying, "Miss you." This has also happened when cord cutting with partners as well. Clients often receive a text, phone call, or email during or right after a session. Time and space do not exist between us. We can feel and sense an energetic disconnection in proximity or miles away; there's no such thing as distance in the energetic field.

This also explains why emotional withdrawal or manipulation can feel as painful as physical abandonment. Emotional detachment disrupts the energetic connection and can be deeply dysregulating.

Chakra Anatomy and Energetic Flow

- The lower chakras are the physical or earthly chakras.
- The upper chakras are the spiritual chakras.
- The heart is the bridge.

The back of the chakras represents the will, and are the place where energy enters to be processed. Trauma and life experiences can create blockages in the back chakras, often resulting in back pain. This area is also a common place for energetic attachments from Spirit. These can be removed by an energy healer or shaman.

The front chakras are emotional and expressive. Many people hold pain or emotion in the back of their body until an "emotional flood" occurs, moving the energy forward into expression.

As we move up the chakra column, the vibration and frequency increase. Scientists have been able to record the sounds of the chakras and discover their tones. These frequencies are based on the solfeggio scale and are used in sound healing to balance and align the chakras. For example: The Root chakra is 396 Hz, and the Crown chakra is 963 Hz.

Sound healing is becoming more widely recognized. Singing bowls, gongs, and tuning forks have shown remarkable effects. Scientists are even shrinking tumors and destroying cancer cells with sound waves. I highly recommend a gong bath or singing-bowl meditation. I finish all my energy sessions with my favorite sound bowl, my clients love it, and so do I.

Kundalini and the Energy Channel

Our chakras connect to our energetic spine, an energetic column extending from the earth up through the body and out the crown. This is the sushumna (in Sanskrit), the channel through which Kundalini energy rises.

Kundalini is our life force energy, often symbolized as a coiled serpent at the base of the spine, lying dormant until it is awakened. When activated, our life force energy rises upward along the sushumna, passing through each chakra. As it ascends, it purifies the chakras. When it reaches the crown, it can result in a spiritual awakening.

A Kundalini awakening can initiate profound spiritual awareness, enhanced intuition, clarity of mind, and a deep sense of purpose. It may culminate in a profound awakened state of bliss, oneness, or emptiness (no-thingness). In the yogic system, this represents the union of Shiva and Shakti, the divine masculine and divine feminine energies merging at the crown. Shakti energy rising up the energetic spine to meet Shiva in the head – becoming divine union. Unity Consciousness.

Last year I had a spiritual experience; a moment of ecstatic bliss in which I saw representations of the divine masculine and divine feminine as a couple seated face to face above me. A spiral of white light wound upwards toward them, ending in a burst of light behind them, resulting in a streaming of white energy downward through me. I was moved to tears. Months later, I read Lama Yeshe's description of a Mahamudra meditation that describes envisioning the divine couple in union above the head - the exact vision I saw. Recently, I have experienced this divine couple descending into my physical body instead of just hovering above it as well. It's a beautiful unity meditation I recommend trying.

Strengthening the Energy Body

Practicing the energy techniques in this book strengthens your energetic system, supporting the awakening of your vital life force. These practices enhance intuition, heighten states of awareness, expand psychic abilities, and may open pathways to awakened states of consciousness, bliss, awakening, and profound spiritual experiences.

Chakra Meditation

By spinning the chakras in a fast, clockwise direction, you spin out anything that has collected in your chakras and increase the vibratory rate of your chakras and your entire energy system. It's a powerful cleansing technique that raises your vibration. This is an excellent tool to use before and during any kind of energy work. It can be especially important if you are working with a client who has cancer, because you need to keep your vibratory frequency above the vibration of the illness being presented.

During this meditation, you will:

Picture the chakra, See the color, Say the color, Spin the chakra fast.

You can do this chakra meditation with or without the corresponding mantras. I recommend first spinning your chakras from 1 through 7 as a standalone exercise. Then, go back through the chakra system again and repeat the mantras for 60 to 180 seconds per chakra. You can also practice these as two separate exercises.

Wheels of Light Meditation

- Find a quiet, comfortable place where you won't be disturbed.
- Sit with a straight spine cross-legged or on a chair with your feet flat on the floor or stand upright to allow energy to flow. Rest your hands in your lap or by your sides.
- Close your eyes and take several deep, relaxing breaths to ground yourself.

Focus on Each Chakra moving from the base upward:

- **Root Chakra (Muladhara):**
- Focus at the base of your spine. Visualize a vibrant red wheel spinning clockwise, very quickly. Chant "Lam," either silently or aloud.
- **Sacral Chakra (Svadhisthana):**
- Shift your awareness just below the navel. Picture a bright orange wheel spinning clockwise. Chant "Vam."
- **Solar Plexus Chakra (Manipura):**

- Move your attention to your upper abdomen. Imagine a brilliant yellow wheel spinning clockwise. Chant "Ram."
- **Heart Chakra (Anahata):**
- Focus on the center of your chest. Visualize a radiant green (or pink) wheel spinning quickly. Chant "Yam."

- **Throat Chakra (Vishuddha):**
- Direct your awareness to your throat. See a sky-blue wheel spinning clockwise. Chant "Ham."
- **Third Eye Chakra (Ajna):**
- Bring your focus to the space between your eyebrows. Visualize an indigo wheel spinning clockwise. Chant "Om."
- **Crown Chakra (Sahasrara):**
- Focus at the top of your head. Picture a brilliant white or violet-white wheel spinning rapidly. Sit in silence or chant "Om."
- Now go back through your entire chakra system, spinning each one clockwise while seeing its color and reciting it.
- When you finish, visualize all seven wheels perfectly aligned, allowing energy to flow freely along your spine.

Take a few deep breaths, return to your body, and gently open your eyes.

Creating Sacred Space

One of the first things I do each morning is create sacred space. I also do this before every session whether online or in person. Creating sacred space is simply the act of being intentional with your environment. It's a way of designating a physical space for spiritual, reflective, or personal practice. Sacred space can be a room, a corner, an outdoor area, or even the energy around your body.

When you create sacred space, you set a protected sanctuary for yourself or for others. My home is my sanctuary, and I'm intentional about how I cultivate its energy for healing, blessing, protection, meditation, and connecting with a higher power. Sacred means holy or "set apart". A space becomes sacred when we have made it so. If you desire to create a sacred space: set a focused intention, and establish the energetic tone you want the space to have.

Each morning, I light a candle and ask Spirit to continue to guide me and support me. I repeat an affirmation twice:

"Infinite Spirit, thank you for opening the divine design operating in my life. For opening the genius in me. I see clearly the perfect plan: health, wealth, love, happiness, and perfect self-expression."

Then I light incense to bless the space. If my intuition tells me the house needs a clearing, I smudge with sage, walking through each room with intention. I repeat:

"My space is cleared of all negativity. Only good energy and good spirit are allowed."

If guided, I do the same with Palo Santo.

I also pull a card of the day for myself. This helps me to be intentional about my day and to live with intention. Then I surrender to the natural flow of intuitive guidance that comes in throughout the day.

Before working with a client, I follow a similar process calling in sacred space, inviting my healing team and theirs, and asking that all information be for the highest and best good. I clear the room energetically before and after each session.

You can personalize your sacred space with objects that hold meaning - candles, plants, crystals, photos, symbols, or anything that helps you feel spiritually aligned.

Energetic Cleansing

As a highly sensitive person and intuitive, clearing my energy and space is essential.

Energetic cleansing removes stagnant or negative energy and brings in higher vibration. You can do this through physical cleaning, opening windows for fresh air, using sound, smudging, or setting an intention. The process aims to create a more balanced and harmonious environment by clearing the space of negative imprints and energy and infusing it with desired positive energy, such as love or protection. Before you begin, state your intention for clearing the space:

"I release all negative energy."

or

"I invite only positive, loving energy into this space."

If there is physical clutter, clear it. Physically clearing clutter allows energy to flow freely. Items from past relationships, unresolved moments, or emotional weight tend to hold energy and don't promote movement. Clean the space - energy settles in corners, on surfaces, and in neglected areas. Fresh air and sunlight naturally lift the vibration of a home and bring in renewed energy.

Burn sage, Palo Santo, or local herbs. Move clockwise through your space, top to bottom or front to back follow your intuition. Remember corners, closets, and entryways; follow your intuition. When you smudge, it's best to have an exit point so the energy leaving has somewhere to go. New items should be cleared as well.

Sound clears energy beautifully - bells, chimes, gongs, singing bowls, or even kirtan music; it lifts the vibe and helps to break up stagnant energy.

Candles also purify a space. Light candles, particularly those made from natural ingredients, and move them through the space, setting intentions for the fire to purify the area. I also burn Epsom salts and grain alcohol. It's amazing. Find a soup bowl with a handle, pour a cup of Epsom salts into the bowl, add a splash or two of grain alcohol, and light it. Be aware and be cautious. This is very hot, will cause a fire if handled improperly, and you will need a trivet to set it on. This combination clears out the toughest energies though!

Crystals can raise and stabilize the vibration of a room:

- Black tourmaline for protection
- Clear quartz to amplify energy
- Selenite to bring high-vibrational light

Surround yourself with what brings you joy; joy is one of the highest vibrational states. If you are in joy, mentally expand that feeling to fill the entire room.

In the end, clearing your space can be as simple as setting an intention. Ask:

"How do I want this space to feel?"

Then follow your intuition. Create your own rituals and make your environment a sanctuary.

How Do We Connect?

Types of Abilities

What's the difference between being intuitive, an empath, a psychic, and a medium?

Being Intuitive

An intuitive person is someone who naturally intuits their environment. They sense the feelings, emotions, moods, and energy of the spaces they're in. Their minds are highly attuned to their surroundings and are constantly gathering information from people, places, and things.

Intuitive individuals tend to be optimistic, introspective, creative, and deeply aware. They often overanalyze and are typically empathic as well. For me, intuition is an inner knowing - those moments when something simply lines up.

For example, I was recently talking with a friend about trees. The next day, someone came up to me excited about a book they were reading about trees. Instantly,

I knew that book was meant for my friend. That's intuition: you just know when something is right.

Being an Empath

The term empath comes from the word empathy and describes a highly sensitive person who can feel and understand the emotions and experiences of others. Empaths don't just sense emotions, they absorb them. You take on what another person is feeling as if it were your own.

Because of this, it's important for empaths to learn cleansing techniques to release energy that isn't theirs. One of the most essential skills is learning to differentiate between your own emotions and the emotions of others. Self-awareness is key. A helpful question to ask yourself is:

"Is this feeling in my body actually mine?"

I remember attending a workshop over ten years ago. Author Dave Markowitz who I later interviewed on my podcast invited a woman on stage who described pain in her stomach. He asked the audience, "Who else feels this pain?" I raised my hand, as did several others. The person sitting next to me whispered, "You can feel that?" and I replied, "You can't?"

That moment showed me how deeply I tune into others and also that not everyone experiences the world the same way.

Empaths take on emotions easily. You can sense the vibe in a room instantly. You understand when someone is upset before they even speak. People tell you their life stories without being asked. You become "the unpaid therapist."

Serious events affect you deeply. Violent or tragic news or movies linger in your body and mind. Pets are drawn to you. Children love you. And you love them.

You may feel physical pain from others before they describe it. Crowds can overwhelm you. You need quiet time to recharge. You're a natural lie detector and you calm people simply by being in the room.

Being Psychic

A psychic can tune into the energy of people, places, and things - sensing information from the past, present, and future. Psychic ability means having extrasensory perception that extends beyond the five physical senses.

Psychic information can come through:

- Clairvoyance (clear seeing)
- Clairaudience (clear hearing)

- Clairsentience (clear feeling)
- Claircognizance (clear knowing)
- And occasionally clairalience (clear smelling) or clairgustance (clear tasting)

Psychic abilities can include astral projection, automatic or channeled writing, divination, dowsing, energy medicine, psychometry, telepathy, telekinesis, remote viewing, and sometimes mediumship. But remember: not all psychics are mediums.

One of my first strong psychic hits came when I was 21. I had just been in a car accident in Simi Valley, California, while visiting a boyfriend. After the accident, I awoke from a dream knowing he had been unfaithful. Later, I found out I was right. That kind of knowing would happen again years later - unsettling and empowering all at once. It reminded me that my intuition had always been speaking; I just needed to listen.

Being a Medium

A medium is a psychic who uses their intuitive abilities to tune specifically into the spirit energy of a person. Mediums communicate with the spirit world, receiving messages from those who have passed. Information comes through the same Clairs - seeing, hearing, feeling, and knowing, but mediumship is unique because it involves communication with the deceased or other nonphysical beings.

All mediums are psychic, but not all psychics are mediums. Being psychic doesn't automatically mean you can see or communicate with spirit.

Recently, I was working with a woman in a mediumship circle. I sensed her brother who had been in a car crash and passed away in the hospital while she sat beside him. In my mind's eye, I saw a mini-movie: the car, the music, the laughter, then the impact. I felt the sensations, the jolt, the pressure and later heard her voice speaking to him in the hospital, seeing her sitting beside him, holding his hand.

What Are the Clairs?

Plus, practices to enhance each ability

Clairvoyance: Clear Seeing

Clairvoyance means "clear seeing." This is the psychic sense of inner sight - receiving intuitive information through mental images or symbolic visions in the mind's eye.

Clairvoyants see internal visions, pictures, images, symbols, or entire mini-movies. These can show:
- A person
- A place
- An event

- The past (retrocognition)
- The future (precognition)
- Auras
- Spirit
- Energy

Some clairvoyants experience outer sight - actually seeing Spirit in the room while others see internally, in their minds eye.

One example from my work:

I once saw a lower leg surgery in my mind's eye and asked a client if they had surgery on their leg. They confirmed they had. Then I saw a young Revolutionary War soldier with a crutch and an amputated leg. Often, current life themes mirror past life experiences that the soul still carries.

This happened to me in my late 20s. After an allergic reaction sent me to the ER, I developed unreasonable fear around food and drinks. The level of fear didn't match the event. A past-life reading later confirmed I had been poisoned in another lifetime. Once I heard this, the fear vanished. Sometimes the soul simply needs to hear:

"That was then. This is now."

I often receive information through memories from my own life. I may see my mother if something relates to a client's mother, or a memory that mirrors their present experience. I'll oftentimes see power animals, angels, or soul fragments waiting to reintegrate.

Clairvoyance can also show historical scenes, like watching a documentary in your mind.

Psychic Practice for Clairvoyance

- Use Zener cards with a partner.
- Practice with playing cards, guessing the next number or suit.

Clairsentience: Clear Feeling

Clairsentience means "clear feeling." This is the psychic sense of feeling energy, emotions, and physical sensations through the body.

A clairsentient can sense:

- Emotions
- Pain
- A person's "vibe"
- Energy in spaces
- The presence of spirit
- The truth behind someone's words
- Physical sensations connected to others

Clairsentience is common among empaths and highly sensitive people. It can be draining, so daily energetic clearing is important.

When I work with a client, I may suddenly feel a stomachache or headache that mirrors theirs. In mediumship, I can feel what a spirit experienced during their passing - pressure in the chest, weakness, or anxiety.

Some people feel Spirit more than they see Spirit. As a child, I turned down my clairvoyance because seeing spirit frightened me, but I could always feel when they were in the room.

Once, while helping at a workshop in an old Seattle home, I saw a woman sitting near a sewing machine in my mind's eye. Later that day, a participant came downstairs saying, "There's an older woman sitting by the sewing machine upstairs." Validating my experience.

Clairsentience can also be physical like feeling a tap on your shoulder when no one is there. As a teenager, I once turned around expecting my sister after feeling a tap... but the room was empty.

Clairsentients often feel like they are a mirror for the world around them. They may feel emotions, pain, or sensations that don't belong to them – like everything they are sensing belongs to someone else. How they read energy may feel like a burden, but it is a gift.

Psychic Practice for Clairsentience

- Psychometry: Hold an object and read its energy.
- Environmental sensing: Walk into different spaces and notice how the energy feels.

Clairalience and Clairgustance: Clear Smelling and Tasting

Clairalience and clairgustance are the clear senses of smell and taste. These abilities involve receiving a psychic sense of taste, which can show up as tasting a flavor or having a memory of a taste arise in your mouth, and receiving a psychic sense of smell, such as cigarette or cigar smoke, perfume, or flowers.

You might smell or taste something that isn't physically present like the scent of roses when an angel or loved one is near, or the smell of cigarette smoke when connecting with a departed relative who smoked.

One time when I was a child, I alerted my parents that I smelled smoke. We'd been watching TV in the living room with a fire going in the fireplace. The fireplace was built into a wall that spanned the center of the house. On the backside of that wall was a closet. My parents told me, "No, that's just the smoke from the fireplace," but I insisted on walking them to where I smelled it and pointed to the closet door. When they opened the closet and felt the wall, it was hot. It turned out the interior of the wall behind the fireplace had caught on fire. There was minimal damage after the fire department broke open the closet wall.

People who have this gift often smell the cologne or perfume of a deceased relative, flowers that aren't there, food that isn't cooking, a particular cleaning product, or even an energetic "scent" like fear or a fishy smell that signals something is off. Psychics have been known to smell death on people or animals when they are close to passing.

Psychic Practice:

- Call in an angel: Sit comfortably, close your eyes, and ask an angel to visit with you. Specifically ask it to send you a smell or taste that isn't physically around you. See if you can smell roses.
- Mediumship: Do a Sitting in the Power meditation and notice whether you sense any smells or tastes from Spirit.

Clairaudience: Clear Hearing

Clairaudience means clear hearing. It's the ability to receive sound through internal hearing.

Clairaudience is the psychic ability to perceive sounds, voices, or music that are not audible to the physical ear. You may hear a word, phrase, tone, or sound that someone standing next to you cannot hear. It can be subtle - a single word, a name, a short phrase, or more extended, like a full sentence or song lyrics.

Clairaudience can also include animal communication. Some people connect with animals, dogs, cats, horses, whales, or other beings by telepathically hearing their messages.

When I'm working with clients, I have audibly heard sounds that relate to their healing process. As a medium, you may hear Spirit speaking in words, phrases, or sounds. Messages often come as a mix of images and inner hearing. For instance, when I heard the phrase, "Are you ready?" that was clairaudience. More recently, while visiting the Pearl Harbor Memorial in Oahu, on the boat ride back to shore I clearly heard a man say, "I'm going home." Heartbreaking, but that too, was clairaudience.

Psychic Practice:

- Listening in public: Sit in a café and softly rest your gaze on one point. Start to tune into different conversations around the room and see if you can isolate one voice or conversation at a time.
- Work with a mentor or group: Join a psychic or mediumship development circle, or work with an experienced teacher to deepen your practice.

Claircognizance: Clear Knowing

Claircognizance, or clear knowing, is the psychic ability of simply knowing something. It's when information suddenly appears in your awareness without any logical way of knowing it. Ideas, insights, or understanding just show up in your mind, seemingly out of nowhere.

Claircognizant people have a direct line to Source Consciousness and receive information directly. You can often tell which Clair is strongest for someone by the words they use:

"I feel..." (clairsentience),

"I see..." (clairvoyance),

or "I know..." (claircognizance).

Because it's often frowned upon in society to "know" things, many people shy away from saying, "I know," and instead soften it to "I feel" or "I think." This means claircognizance is one of the most overlooked gifts, simply because of language and conditioning. Yet claircognizant people regularly receive sudden insights, instant downloads, and a deep sense of truth without evidence. Words, ideas, inspirations, song lyrics, and realizations just pop into their mind.

You might think of a friend and then see them or receive a call. You might text someone only to have them reply, "I was just thinking of you!"

When I'm working with a client, claircognizance often comes before they arrive. I'll suddenly feel the urge to clean my house top to bottom, and when the client shows up, she says, "I've been cleaning everything out at home." That's claircognizance, an instant knowing that mirrors what's happening around you.

This ability shows up as certainty: you know when something is right or wrong, when someone isn't being truthful, or when something significant has occurred in a space or with a person. On one occasion, my now ex-husband and I were doing a walkthrough of a rental house. When we walked into the primary bedroom, I had the thought: squatter. I asked the woman showing us the home if someone had been squatting there. She said yes and asked how I could possibly know that.

Telepathy lives in this realm. Telepathy is the gift of receiving information instantly in your mind the transfer of thoughts, emotions, or images between individuals without speech or physical senses. It's a form of extrasensory perception (ESP), like precognition.

As I shared earlier, I often joke that you can be quietly thinking, I really want pizza, and your child walks in and says, "Can we have pizza for dinner?" It's a simple thought that happens to match exactly what someone near you is thinking.

Or you may get the clear thought: My client is going to cancel tomorrow, and the next day you receive a text confirming it. Telepathic knowing isn't usually a long, dramatic monologue in your head; it's often a simple, clean, precise thought. It's communication simplified beyond time and space. You can receive information across great distances; proximity doesn't matter. Emotional or intimate connection strengthens the link.

While proofreading this book, I listened to an episode of The Telepathy Tapes podcast (Season 2, Episode 4), where guest Jason Padgett shared his view on the science of telepathy. Padgett said:

"It's entanglement, just information that's being entangled from the boundary of the event horizon to the singularity. The entanglement of light."

Wikipedia describes quantum entanglement as a phenomenon in which the quantum state of each particle in a group cannot be described independently of the state of the others. Padgett goes on to explain that entanglement allows us to understand what's happening in another person's brain by seeing the reflection of it. Theoretically, we can retrieve information from anywhere in the universe instantaneously.

Someone with strong telepathy has stronger entanglement. We feel separate, but fundamentally we are all "on top of each other" in the information field. When a telepath and the person they're tuning into reach a kind of coherence, when the "angle" of the light information matches, there is quantum teleportation of information. In other words, when quantum states reach a coherence threshold, information transfers non-locally through entanglement.

If you think telepathy looks like hearing an entire conversation in your head, like in the movies, that hasn't been my experience. For me, it's a single, clear thought that arrives in my mind often when I'm near someone, emotionally connected to them, or about to interact with them, such as a scheduled client. It can be local or nonlocal. Whether I'm in the same room or across the world doesn't really matter. For me, there is no such thing as distance, I receive information regardless of proximity.

Just like the empath must learn to differentiate between which feelings are theirs and which are not, the claircognizant must learn to differentiate between which thoughts are theirs and which are not. A claircognizant person may feel like their mind is "not their own," or that they're constantly picking up other people's thoughts.

Each of the Clairs represents a different channel of intuitive communication. You may have one dominant Clair or several working together. The key is to notice how your intuition speaks to you and to trust it when it does.

Intuition is very "in the moment." When you ask a question, the answer often arrives before you even finish the sentence. You think of someone, and they call. You consider taking a dance class, and an email or ad appears for a local studio. You speak a desire aloud and the answer comes through a friend, a message, or social media. You realize you need something for your house and then see it sitting on the side of the road for free.

Once you truly tap in, the possibilities are endless—and your manifestation capacity increases. When you get into a true flow with the universe, you may find you have to start watching what you say and think, because your words and thoughts manifest quickly. Life becomes a magical co-creation with the universe.

Psychic Practice:

- Third eye focus: During meditation, bring your awareness to the space between your eyebrows. Use this as a focal point for receiving insights and inner knowing as you listen.
- Random "knowing" practice: Ask a simple question about your day (e.g., "Who will contact me next?" or "Which elevator door will open first?"). Notice the first thought that pops into your mind then watch how often it turns out to be right.

Signs, Symbols, Synchronicities, and Coincidences

Signs, symbols, synchronicities, and coincidences are how our environment, the universe, and Spirit communicate with us. They are reminders that we are supported, guided, and loved- little hints and breadcrumbs along our path to help us through life. These moments show us we're not alone, that something is right or wrong, and that everything will be okay.

Let's go through some of the ways these signs might appear.

Messages From Spirit

From Spirit, you may receive butterflies or birds. It's very common for family members who have passed on to send butterflies, birds, feathers, and similar gifts. These "spirit winks" let us know they're still with us. The sign is often personal - maybe a bird your mother loved or a butterfly connected to a childhood memory.

It might be a hummingbird that suddenly flies up to your face while you're gardening or a cardinal that lands near your window. Many people find feathers after difficult times. I still find them often. They've become quiet reminders that I'm supported and that everything is all right.

Songs and Sound

You might also receive messages through music. In my book *Mom Died Last Night*, I share how, after my mother passed away, she communicated with me through song lyrics I'd hear as I was waking up. I would also hear perfectly timed songs on the radio that lined up with what I was experiencing or what I was about to do.

One day I was driving to meet a friend who wanted to talk about something important. I turned on the radio, and the song that came on right before I arrived was, Can We Just Talk.

When something like that happens, pay attention. It's not random. Look up the lyrics; sometimes a single line carries the message. One morning, I woke up with one lyric repeating in my mind, and it ended up being completely relevant to what I was about to experience that day.

Everyday Signs

Signs can also come through practical, everyday moments - an unexpected email, a message from a friend, or something you scroll past online. For example, if you're researching a health concern, a friend might suddenly mention a book or remedy that perfectly fits what you've been wondering about.

These are what I call angel messages, Spirit speaking through other people to deliver love, reassurance, or direction.

Numbers and Patterns

Another common form of synchronicity is repeating numbers: 111, 222, 333, 10:10, 12:12, and so on. I call them angel numbers. Each sequence has its own meaning, for example – 12:12 stands for spiritual growth and awakening. If you start seeing 1:11, Spirit is trying to show you that there's more to life than meets the eye.

I Google their meanings all the time, you can too. When I see them, I always take note of what I was thinking in that exact moment. The message almost always connects to my situation.

Objects and Tokens

You might find a small object that connects to someone you love. One friend of mine had recently lost someone dear to her. While driving home, she noticed a small angel statue sitting in a box on the side of the road. The moment she saw it, the person she had lost came to mind, and she knew it was a sign.

When these moments happen, a particular person or situation usually pops into your mind instantly, that's how you know who the message is from.

Dreams and Visitations

Dreams are another beautiful way Spirit communicates. They can hold signs, symbols, messages, and even direct visitations. Sometimes you'll dream about something unfolding in your life, and other times you may experience a dream visitation, a loved one, guide, or Spirit giving reassurance or guidance.

I once dreamed that a woman - whom I believe was one of my guides - approached me and simply said, "Liz, you're going to be okay." It was a clear, direct message that brought deep peace during a difficult time.

Recognizing the Connection

You'll often just know when a sign is meant for you. Pay attention to what you were thinking, feeling, or doing in that moment.

- Did a memory surface when you saw the butterfly?
- Did you think of your grandmother when the bird appeared?
- Did a song play that instantly reminded you of your father?

These are all ways Spirit and the universe speak.

The more you acknowledge these signs, the more they appear. Synchronicities grow stronger when you pay attention, it becomes a beautiful dialogue between you and the divine.

Pay attention. Have fun with it. See how many signs, symbols, coincidences, and synchronicities show up in your life. Watch how Spirit continues to find ways to show you that you are loved, guided, and never alone.

Dream Time

I love dream time. I keep a dream journal next to my bed, and most of the time I try write down whatever I can remember. Sometimes it's just a snippet, and other times I'm lucky enough to recall the whole dream.

Dreams are fascinating because you can dive into them and start to apply them to your life experiences and understanding of yourself. I keep a dream dictionary beside my bed, and there are plenty of online resources that explain dream interpretation.

We do a lot of personal processing in our dreams. Many reflect what's going on in our lives, our emotions, experiences, and daily events. But some dreams go beyond that. They can be intuitive or precognitive, revealing what's unfolding or what's to come. Dreaming is another way intuition speaks.

Writing dreams down allows you to track what you're processing, what's happening now, and what may be coming in the future. It's amazing to look back and see how dreams speak to you.

I recommend keeping a dream journal next to your bed with a pen so you can jot down even the smallest detail. Sometimes that tiny fragment gives you a big clue about what's going on.

And then there are precognitive dreams, those magical moments when you realize, "Wow, I saw that coming". Maybe you dreamed of a house before moving into it, or a person you would later meet. These moments remind us that intuition comes in many forms.

If you have trouble remembering dreams, set an intention before bed and repeat it a few times as you fall asleep. Ask your angels or guides to help you remember. You can even ask a direct question:

"Angels and guides, please show me insight about this situation in my dreams tonight."

Sometimes you'll get an answer; sometimes you won't. But when you do, it's incredible.

I like to write little notes beneath my dream entries once I look up the symbols or see what they corresponded to. It's fun to go back later and see the patterns and how often they match what was happening at the time. Or when you were precognitive dreaming.

Another thing I've started doing is writing down my morning musings, the thoughts that come right after waking. Lately, I've noticed that my morning thoughts often match what I experience during the day, both personally and with clients. It feels like a download of what's to come. The more I pay attention, the more I realize I'm receiving information all the time.

Give yourself a few minutes in the morning to let your mind wander. See if your thoughts correlate with your day. It's been a worthwhile practice for me.

Add These
to Your Journal!

If you haven't yet, grab yourself a notebook something small enough to fit in your purse or glove compartment, or one you can keep beside your bed. Make it something easy to carry so it's always nearby.

Start paying attention to all the signs, symbols, synchronicities, and coincidences that show up in your life.

Write down:

- Songs that catch your attention
- Animals or birds you notice
- Feathers you find
- "Right place, right time" moments
- Things people suddenly say that feel like messages
- Anything that feels like a nudge, wink, or whisper

Write it all down.

Maybe an animal reminds you of your grandmother, or a bird makes you think of your grandfather. Maybe you find a feather after asking for guidance. Record it so you can start to see how often the universe speaks to you.

Also pay attention to your dreams:

- Vivid dreams
- Meaningful dreams
- Dreams you can't forget
- Visitations
- Repeating symbols
- Significant places or people

Your journal becomes a map of how Spirit communicates with you. Over time, you'll start to recognize your unique intuitive language.

Keep your notebook with you so you can jot things down anytime, anywhere because signs and synchronicities can appear at any moment.

If you're ever unsure, just ask. It's okay to ask for a sign. Then watch what happens.

I remember once telling my mother about angels. Before we walked into a plant nursery, we said, "Angels, please give us a sign that you're with us." As we entered, a woman walked up, looked at my baby with bright white-blonde hair, and said, "Oh, look at that angel hair." It was simple and perfect.

So, watch for the signs. Notice the birds and butterflies. Pay attention to the numbers on the clock, what were you thinking when you saw them? Listen to what people say around you; Spirit often speaks through others. When the message is meant for you, you'll feel it.

Write everything down.

At the end of the week, look back through your notes and see how many signs and synchronicities you received. What were they? How did they make you feel? How are they shaping your life?

Write it down. Reflect. And watch what happens.

Becoming Aware

Intention

An intention is something we intend - something we consciously choose to create or act upon. It's an action plan for how we want to move through life.

So how do we go about setting an intention, and why is it important?

Intentions matter because they give us focus. They clarify what we want to experience and create. To intend something, for me, means to consciously bring something into being - to manifest it in my life.

I set intentions for my day, my week, my month, and my future. It's a way of aligning myself with what I want to call in. We could simply go through life letting things happen to us, but why not seize the opportunity to become creative with our life? Why not co-create with the universe and manifest our best possible reality?

This is why we set intentions. When we intend for our life to unfold in a certain way, we become active participants in creating it. Intention puts us in the driver's seat of our own experience.

Setting Intentions

Simple ways to set intentions include doing so first thing in the morning during meditation. When you wake up, take a moment to decide what you want your morning, your day, or even your week to look like. Visualize it clearly. You can also set broader intentions for your month, your year, or your future.

When we set intentions, we're focusing our attention on what we want, and the universe responds to where we place that attention whether positive or negative.

The Power of Attention

The universe gives us what we focus on. Personally, I'd rather use that power to manifest positivity, things that uplift me and align with my purpose than simply let life "just happen."

That doesn't mean we stop surrendering and trusting the natural flow of life. But the universe wants us to participate. We are creator beings, and where our attention goes, our energy flows.

If we're stuck on the hamster wheel of life, focusing on negative thoughts, that's where our attention and therefore our energy goes. We end up creating more of that same vibration. We start telling a story about our life that keeps repeating itself.

So, let's flip that.

Let's set intentions that are clear and aligned with what we truly want. Let's place our attention on the life we choose to create. When we do, we begin to manifest that better day, that better week, that better month, that better year.

Setting intentions is about becoming aware, paying attention to what we're thinking, how we're feeling, and what we're envisioning for our future.

Let's set our intentions, pay attention to them, and consciously co-create with the universe.

Exercise: Setting Intentions

This week, I want you to work with intention to become conscious of what you are calling into your life.

1.Create a quiet space.

Find a few moments each morning or evening to sit quietly. Take three deep breaths. Feel yourself become present in your body and connected to your heart.

2. Ask yourself:

- What do I want to experience today?
- How do I want to feel?
- What would I like to create or attract into my life right now?

Write it down.

In your journal, begin with the words:

"Today I intend..."

or

"I am ready to..."

Write freely. Your intention might be as simple as, "I intend to stay calm and grounded," or as expansive as, "I intend to open myself to new opportunities aligned with my purpose."

4.Bring attention to your intention.

Throughout your day, pause and gently remind yourself of what you intended. Notice where your thoughts and feelings are focused, this is where your creative energy is flowing. If you drift into worry or distraction, simply return your attention to your intention.

5.Reflect.

At the end of the day or week, look back at your journal.

- Did your experiences reflect your intention?
- How did you feel when you held that focus?
- What small synchronicities or changes did you notice?

6.Express gratitude.

Give thanks for the clarity, lessons, and manifestations that arose. Gratitude amplifies energy and opens the flow for more of what you desire.

Remember: Intention + Attention = Creation.

You are a powerful co-creator with the universe. The more you practice setting and honoring your intentions, the more naturally your outer world will begin to reflect your inner vision.

Having Awareness

We've now explored intention and attention, now let's talk about awareness.

Awareness is your focus. It is your intention. It is your attention. It's the clarity you bring to where you are directing your energy and what you are choosing to perceive. Awareness is about being receptive, open to receive, and consciously noticing what's unfolding within and around you.

Setting the intention to be fully aware in each moment means being awake to everything: to your morning, to other people's emotions, to the energy of a room, to the feeling of a business you walk into. It's having awareness of yourself, your emotions, your thoughts, your patterns, and your belief systems.

All of these layers of awareness point you toward creating the life you desire. To live in intuitive flow, you must first be aware of your own abilities and of your everyday energy.

Bring awareness to your thoughts during the day. Notice your feelings in different situations. Tune in to the subtle information you receive all the time. The more you practice this, the more fully you'll understand yourself, how you work, how your intuition speaks, and how your energy interacts with the world.

Everyone experiences intuition differently. Awareness is the journey of self-discovery that allows you to understand your unique language with Spirit. Through awareness, you begin to see:

- How your feelings guide you
- Where your wounds and belief systems shape your perceptions
- How your thought processes influence what you create

Ask yourself:

- How am I receiving information?
- Am I noticing signs, coincidences, or synchronicities?
- Are my thoughts pointing me toward something the universe wants me to see?
- What am I seeing, hearing, feeling, tasting, or sensing?

This is awareness, observing how your intuitive messages arrive.

For me, awareness often shows up as images from my own life that act as clues to what's happening for my clients, friends, or family. That's how my intuition speaks. Pay attention to how yours communicates.

Have awareness around your patterns of receiving. Keep journaling. Meditate. This is where the real work lies, getting to know yourself deeply.

Know thyself.

Awareness, intention, and attention all work together as part of this process. So be aware. Be focused. Look within. Watch what's unfolding around you. Step into the flow and know yourself.

Exercise: A Day of Awareness

This week, I invite you to practice living with awareness.

1.Begin your day with intention.

When you wake up, take a few deep breaths. Set the intention to be fully aware throughout your day. You might say something like:

"Today, I intend to be present and aware of what I see, hear, and feel."

2.Notice your inner world.

Throughout the day, pay attention to your thoughts, emotions, and physical sensations. What do you notice when you walk into a room? How do certain people or places make you feel? If your energy shifts, take a moment to pause and ask yourself why.

3.Observe your outer world.

Be mindful of the signs, symbols, and synchronicities around you. Maybe a song catches your attention, a feather crosses your path, or a friend says exactly what you needed to hear. These are moments of communication from Spirit and the Universe.

4.Journal your awareness.

Keep a small notebook with you, or make a note in your phone. Record the things that stand out the sensations, the emotions, the patterns, and the intuitive hits. At the end of the day, review your notes and reflect on what themes appeared.

5.Reflect and integrate.

Ask yourself:

- What did I notice about myself today?
- What emotions or thoughts kept repeating?
- Did I feel guided or supported in any way?

- How did awareness shift my choices or perspective?

6.End your day with gratitude.

Before you go to sleep, take a moment to thank yourself for paying attention. Awareness strengthens intuition, and every time you practice it, you deepen your connection to your higher self and the world around you.

Awareness is presence in motion. The more you bring your awareness into each moment, the more clearly, you'll begin to see the guidance that's always been there, quietly waiting for you to notice.

Trusting Yourself

This is work.

It's the work of an intuitive, a sensitive, and especially of an empath, because when you're constantly picking up on other people's energy, you have to learn how to tell what's yours and what's someone else's. And part of that process is trust.

Learning to trust your intuition is part of the inner work. It was a huge part of my work.

When we're growing up, a lot of doubt gets created. Maybe, like me, you often heard, "Are you sure?" Those three words can plant seeds of uncertainty. Hearing them repeatedly teaches us to doubt ourselves and creates a lack of confidence in our own inner knowing.

As children, we also learn to look outside ourselves for validation. We look to our parents "Am I making the right decision?" and often they make it for us. We learn to let circumstances or the opinions of others shape our choices. Over time, we stop counting on ourselves. We give away our power - lose touch with our autonomy and sovereignty.

What Trust Looks Like

Trust looks like getting that gut feeling and following it. It's listening to your intuition and taking the next step, even when you're unsure of the outcome. It's having faith in your ability to make a clear, conscious decision without doubting yourself.

And of course, we all doubt. We all wonder, "Am I making the right choice?".

I think that's one of the reasons psychics and intuitives are in such demand - we crave certainty. We want someone else to confirm what we already feel but don't yet trust.

If you were raised to trust yourself, that's wonderful. But most of us weren't. We were taught to depend on parents, teachers, caregivers, and to look outside for answers. The work now is to bring that faith back into yourself.

Trusting yourself means reclaiming your ability to make clear decisions on your own. It means standing in your autonomy, free from the need for external approval or validation. It's no longer about what others think; it's about what feels true to you.

Building Self-Trust

When you have a gut feeling, an intuitive nudge, or an idea, don't immediately look to someone else for confirmation. Don't ask, what will they think? or What if I'm wrong?

Just follow it. See what happens.

Start with baby steps. We've spent so much of our lives doubting our decision-making process that rebuilding self-trust takes time. It's a day by day, step by step process of practicing, noticing, and allowing.

Give yourself permission to trust yourself.

Set the intention to follow your intuition. Pay attention to your inner guidance and allow yourself to have faith in your own wisdom. And most importantly, allow yourself the opportunity to make mistakes. Not every intuitive hit will open the right door. Sometimes you'll find closed ones. That's okay.

It's all part of learning to trust.

The key is to keep showing up to set the intention, pay attention, and take each small step forward in faith. Let yourself flow with your own rhythm. Look at your feelings and thoughts. Listen to your inner voice. And stop counting on everyone else to tell you what's right.

Because trusting yourself is the foundation of intuitive living and it always begins within you.

Exercise: Building Self-Trust

This week, I want you to practice trusting yourself your intuition, your feelings, and your inner knowing.

1.Set the intention.

Before you start your day, take a quiet moment to say to yourself:

"Today, I choose to trust myself. I choose to listen to my intuition and follow what feels true."

Breathe deeply and feel that intention settle into your heart.

2.Notice your inner signals.

Throughout the day, pay attention to the small nudges you receive.

- Do you suddenly feel like calling someone?
- Are you drawn to go somewhere or do something unexpected?

- Does something inside whisper yes or no?

These are your intuitive signals.

3.Take a small step.

When you feel one of those nudges, follow it. Take one small action without second-guessing or asking anyone's opinion. It might be as simple as turning left instead of right, sending that message, or saying what's really on your heart.

4.Reflect and record.

At the end of the day, write in your journal:

- What intuitive hit did I follow today?
- How did it feel to trust myself?
- What happened when I listened?
- How did I feel when I doubted myself?

Be honest and compassionate, this is a practice, not a test.

5.Celebrate your wins.

Even the smallest moments of trust count. Every time you honor your intuition, you strengthen your confidence and your connection with your higher self.

6.If you miss a cue, don't judge yourself.

There will be days when you doubt or ignore that inner voice and that's okay. Awareness is progress. Simply notice it, forgive yourself, and try again.

Trust grows in the space between listening and action. Each time you follow your intuition, you prove to yourself that you can be trusted and that your inner guidance is real, reliable, and always leading you where you need to be.

Conclusion

Live Your Intuitive Life.

Thank you so much for joining me on this adventure learning about your intuition, how to use it, and how to live a better, more aligned life.

I truly believe that living from your intuitive guidance gives you the ability to live your best life. It has brought me joy, peace, and a deeper sense of purpose. By following my intuition, I always find myself stepping into the next best thing meant for me.

I love my life, and I know you will too when you begin to notice the signs, symbols, coincidences, and synchronicities – the magic unfold. When you're fully tuned in to your intuition when you understand how it works and how you personally receive information, you begin to know yourself on a deeper level. You become more balanced, grounded, and centered. You develop awareness around your gifts, your energy, and how you want to express them in the world.

Now it's time to take everything you've learned and go out there and live your intuitive life – your best life.

Set your intentions. Pay attention. Live intentionally.

Be aware of your aura, how you're functioning in the world, how you're communicating with the universe, and how you're co-creating your reality. Have awareness of your chakras and of what you're feeling, seeing, hearing, and knowing. Notice what you pick up from other people and from your environment, these are all clues.

Pay attention to what you're receiving. Notice your Clairs, how you receive information and how it shows up for you. Watch how it all unfolds.

When you bring awareness to these things, you step into flow and the flow of life is exactly where you want to be.

It's trusting yourself.

It's trusting your gut instinct.

It's trusting your inner knowing and your five senses -and everything beyond them.

You already have what you need. You just need to bring your awareness to it. Use your inner voice. Use your inner guidance system.

Intend to live this way. Pay attention. Enjoy it. Enjoy the magic of how intuition shows up in your life. When you do, you'll be living your best, most authentic, joy filled life.

I promise you.

I'm so excited for you, because this work excites me. This is the magic of life, and I want you to feel that same magic too.

So do the exercises. Practice the practices. Pay attention. Set your intentions. And live your best life now.

Thank you for joining me on this journey. It has been an honor and a joy to walk beside you.

Live from your intuition. Live a life in flow. Live your best life. Today.

About the Author

A seer, seeker, and spiritual explorer, Liz Peterson is an author, trained Intuitive Energy Healer, Reiki Master, Spiritual Coach, and podcaster. Liz has been a lifelong student of healing, personal growth, and metaphysics. She is the host of the podcast Raise the Vibe with Liz, dedicated to bringing today's inspirational speakers, way showers, and ascension leaders to an international audience. Her podcast mission is simple: to heal the world, one guest at a time.

A mother of four, Liz lives on a small island in the Pacific Northwest, where she enjoys peaceful surroundings and the beauty of nature. She brings years of training, natural intuitive abilities, and her own personal journey of healing, transformation, and empowerment to her work with individuals.

With love and compassion, it is her mission to assist others on their spiritual journey of awakening and healing. Liz empowers and guides people to clear and release stuck energy, blocks, and trauma while activating the body's natural healing process.

You can find her offerings at:
www.raisethevibewithliz.com